A guide to vintage guitar collecting

How to get started, build and maintain a guitar collection with advice and personal commentary from the leading collectors and authorities around the world

by Bill Blackburn, Ph.D.
Foreword by James Werner

Cover Photo: James Werner, in what has come to be known as the "Totally Awesome" shot, circa 1983.
Photographer-W.D. Lewis III; Layout-Angela Marchionno; Paste-up-Wes Middlebrook; Production-Ron Middlebrook

SAN 683-8022
ISBN 0-931759-60-9

The information presented in this guide represents the opinions of the author and the subjective accounts of the collectors surveyed. All recommendations and suggestions are made without any guarantee on the part of the author or publisher, who also must disclaim any liability incurred in relationship to the use of the information presented in this guide. The author and the publisher acknowledge that some words, brand names, model names and designations are the property of the trademark holder. These terms are necessarily used for identification purposes. This work does not constitute an official publication of any of the guitar makers referred to.

Copyright 1992 William D. Blackburn

Published by CENTERSTREAM Publishing
P.O. Box 5450 - Fullerton, CA 92635
ALL RIGHTS RESERVED

Dedicated to the memory and the creations of Leo Fender

CONTENTS

Foreword by James Werner 4
Acknowledgments 5
Introduction 6
    Getting Started
        a. History of Guitar Collecting 8
        b. Vintage Instruments 8
        c. What to Collect 9
        d. Fun or Profit 10
    Why Do We Go Nuts for Vintage Guitars?
        (Guitar Collector Survey, Report 1,) 12
    Building a Collection
        a. Gathering Knowledge 20
        b. Guitar Identification 20
        c. Where to Look 21
        d. What to Buy 23
    Sometimes a Guitar Is Just a Guitar
        (Guitar Collector Survey, Report 2,) 27
    Guitar Terminology 36
    The Thrill of Vintage and The Agony of Defret
        (Guitar Collector Survey, Report 3,) 45
    Maintaining Your Collection 52
        a. Basics 52
        b. Storage and Security 52
        c. Restoration 53
        d. Miscellany 54
    Afterwords
        (Guitar Collector Survey, "Update" Report 4,) 55
Appendix A
    Guitar Collector Questionnaire 71
Appendix B
    Be-Bop-A-Black Strat 74
Appendix C
    Guitar Collector Questionnaire (Update) 80
Bibliography 83

FOREWORD

Since I have become a legend in my own mind, initially I had declined to do this forward. However, I am possibly the best known unknown collector and might represent others in the field, so - - -

The following pages are about old guitar collecting from the <u>basics</u> approach of starting, maintaining and continuing the acquisition of vintage guitars. Topics include communication hygiene, terminology and grading, information sources, and insight by established collectors.

The interviews with these well known collectors tell how they started, give placement of values and pet peeves, plus projections of future collectibles. An unusual aspect is the merging of Dr. Blackburn's professional background in the mental health field with his interest in collecting and explaining why we collect. Once inflicted with Sunburst Satyriasis, there is no cure! There is vital information for both the novice and the experienced preserver of the past.

That guy on the cover - - didn't he used to be nearly famous and almost humble?

James Werner
Letts, Iowa

ACKNOWLEDGMENTS

I would first like to thank **Noë Goldwasser** for his initial support of my theme when he was Editor-in-Chief of Guitar World magazine. His approval and guidance were critical to the initiation of the "Guitar Collector Survey." From my early conversations with guitarist **Mark Chatfield** and first (long) phone call with **James Werner**, Fender collector, I began to experience the genuine enthusiasm that existed for the instruments and the friendly encouragement that other collectors could provide. I wish to sincerely express my appreciation to all of the guitar collectors who contributed their time and expertise to this project. Their willingness to devote their energies and share their knowledge and experiences have made this work possible. Without the collectors' comments, this book would literally not exist.

James Werner proved to be the guiding inspiration for this project. His resources were essential to the survey, and his friendship and altruistic posture served as powerful motivators to see the book through to completion. Many of the survey participants have been especially helpful; among them are: **George Gruhn** for his involvement from the first article to the last chapter, and review of parts of the manuscript, **Vic Da Pra** and **Tim Matyas** for their friendship, positive attitudes and photographic contributions, **John Peden** for permission to use his candid shot of **Steve Melkisethian** and his "Collector's Choice" photo of the Howard Reed Strat, **Ron Lira** for his assistance with the guitar storage section, **Jay Scott** for his selection and definitions of Gretsch terms, **Brian Fischer** for the photos of his collection, and **André Duchossoir**, **Richard Smith** and **Tom Van Hoose** for their thoughtful editorial contributions.

Many individuals besides the collectors have been invaluable to this work; among them are: **Bill Clark** for his legal advice, **Ron Middlebrook** of Centerstream for his patience and assistance in structuring my articles into this collecting guide, **Bill Barbour** for his insights on the subject of design as art, and **Lis Rundle** for her word processing and editing talents.

I would also like to thank **Cindy**, **Abbey** and the other "guitar widows" who have exercised infinite patience and understanding in the service of the preservation and appreciation of vintage guitars, in other words - - tolerating their guitar crazed partners.

INTRODUCTION

In the early 1980's I was finishing my doctoral degree in psychology at The Ohio State University. I continued, and do to this day, my clinical work with children, families and adults, but for the first time in a decade I was able to expand my single-minded pursuit of academic, career and family related necessities. My reference to "single-minded" identifies a mental disposition that attempts to resist diversions, which may interfere with a specific goal directed activity. Such avoidance of fun was purposeful, but not entirely rewarding.

My interests, and attentions, returned (without the guilt) to my early love of guitars and amps. I was one of thousands of baby boomers that became fascinated with guitars and guitar music during the first British invasion of the Beatles and Stones. I had enjoyed a couple of guitars and amps around the house over the years, but had not "allowed" myself to consider musical ventures for a long time. As I began to explore the purchase of another guitar, my rejection of new instruments was predictable as I regressed to my adolescent pursuits of sunburst Les Pauls and early Fenders. The original "Bursts" remained elusive, but I soon became seriously, compulsively involved in Fender collecting. It was thrilling, but somehow frightening, how quickly the initial "symptoms" of what I was later to term "Old Guitar Mania" (OGM) developed.

At about this same time I had discovered Guitar World magazine which further exacerbated my condition by their focus on vintage guitars, specifically their "Collector's Choice" guitar centerfolds. In March, 1984, I wrote to Noë Goldwasser who was at that time Editor-in-Chief of Guitar World. I was writing to congratulate Noë on his work and query him about my interest in writing an article on the psychology of guitar collecting. Fortunately, Noë was supportive of my idea. Having just completed my doctoral research, I concluded that more "data" was needed than my own subjective experiences. I had become fascinated with the intensity of the collecting fever and hoped to study the development and course of the phenomenon in others. This led to the construction of the "Guitar Collector Questionnaire" (Appendix A) and subsequent first article for Guitar World, "Why Do We Go Nuts For Vintage Guitars?"

The "Guitar Collector Survey" was not, of course, a strictly scientific survey, but rather a voluntary sampling of many of the most respected names in the collecting field, and dedicated enthusiasts from the United States and Europe. The rock star collectors proved disinterested in participating, but the others were extremely generous with their time and expertise. Their comments and contributions are the heart of this work.

My communications and relationships with the other collectors were to become as valuable as the guitars themselves. As in "group therapy," it is truly an emotionally satisfying and therapeutic experience to find individuals that possess your same feelings and interests. Such normalizing ("I'm not the only nut") encounters are very valuable psychologically. The guitar collecting passion allows fluent discussions and personal connections between individuals from diverse backgrounds. Educational and cultural differences are lost in the context of "Bursts," "Strats," and "Custom Colors."

It was also exciting to find that the guitar collecting hobby has generational ties to a large extent and serves to anchor an individual with his or her peer group. Most of the survey participants are now in their thirties and forties and grew up during the same times. These "middle age" individuals are ready developmentally to look back and capture some part of their vanishing youth, whether it be a sixties muscle car or a '59 Burst. These generational ties also facilitate relationships between the collectors.

Some years after I had completed the third unpublished "report," "The Thrill of Vintage and the Agony of Defret," from the Guitar Collector Survey, I began talking to Ron Middlebrook of Centerstream Publications. I was determined to find a source to publish the third article and ideally to include the others also. Ron suggested that I write additional chapters to develop a guide to vintage guitar collecting. The present work is the result. While I am a psychologist, I do not consider myself a vintage guitar expert, per se. I believe you will find this work to be unbalanced on the side of the psychological and aesthetic rather than the financial or practical. Such reflects my own bias and perspective. Hopefully, my primary theme of appreciation and respect for the old guitars will be evident in my writing. The practical aspects of this guide are relegated to the basics and were garnered largely from my own experiences and information from survey participants. I hope the beginning collector will find the information useful. While such practical guidance is obvious to the seasoned collector, I trust such individuals will be informed and entertained by the advice and personal commentary from the leading collectors and authorities that have generously contributed to the project.

I first entered the guitar collecting world as a teenager seeking my "dream guitar." Having survived an early middle age episode of OGM, I continue to collect Fender guitars and "black face" Fender amps.

Bill Blackburn
Worthington, Ohio

GETTING STARTED

History of Guitar Collecting

Guitar collecting, for the most part, is a relatively recent phenomenon, when compared to other established categories of collectibles and antiques. There has likely always been a limited interest in the collection of ancient instruments, but most of the guitars that are sought after presently are only twenty-five to sixty-five years old.

Guitar collecting as it exists today had its origins in the search for proper instruments throughout the sixties. As George Gruhn (vintage guitar authority and survey participant) has observed, the first wave of interest in older guitars occurred during the early sixties in relationship to the widespread acceptance of folk music. By the end of the rock music explosion of the mid- to late sixties, the preference for a group of vintage (at that time simply "used") guitars was nearly established.

The first collectors were interested in acoustic instruments: flat top guitars that were produced before World War II, as well as arch top guitars from the mid-1920's through the mid-1960's. Many collectors continue to focus on the acoustics and consider them to be the prime collectibles, but the guitars that are prized by most of the survey participants are American made electrics of the 1950's and 1960's. These mid-century electrics represent an especially memorable period in guitar history, and an equally memorable period in the lives of many collectors.

Most of the guitar collectors thus surveyed were born during the 1940's and 1950's. These children of the baby boom were teenagers or pre-teens during this special time in guitar development. Actually, this was an especially prolific period in overall American manufacturing. After World War II, American companies turned their focus to the manufacturing of consumer goods again with highly collectible results due to the quantity and quality of items as well as the great present day nostalgic appeal. Thousands of near middle age individuals collect furniture, clothing, and memorabilia from this period. But, a guitar is more than an Eames chair, a Hawaiian shirt or even a Davy Crockett hat. While many collectible items possess some degree of utility value, few could claim the importance that an instrument has in the life of the musician.

The selection of the specific electric guitars that were destined to become the future collectibles was largely determined by the choices of the most popular guitarists of the day playing primarily in the blues rock area. Of course, Bloomfield, Beck, Clapton and the like were able to recognize the merits of certain instruments and used them accordingly. Such latter day widespread acceptance and desirability of specific guitars certainly is more complicated than simple hero worship. For example, if you desired the distinctive sound and character of a sunburst Les Paul Standard in the late sixties, there was arguably no substitute and the guitar was not being produced at the time. Thus, many aspiring baby booming guitarists of the day had no choice but to seek out the original, and many of them are still searching!

Vintage Instruments

What is a vintage guitar? There is not a simple answer for this seemingly straightforward question. Some guitars, like wine, may improve with age, or at least some models become more desirable with the passage of time. No two collectors are likely to agree on the determination of which guitars are collectible. Over the last twenty years or so, only a limited number of guitars manufactured by a handful of American companies have by convention established themselves as truly collectible. A guitar does not become collectible just because it is old or even rare.

Of course, virtually any guitar is, in principle, a collectible item. But, until a specific guitar develops a following to some degree, its value may remain only in the view of its collector. It is difficult to provide a comprehensive list of the most accepted collectors' guitars due to fluctuation and trends in the field. A guitar that was very desirable last year may have cooled off considerably, or may no longer be of interest at all to the collector. Everyone is familiar with the names of a limited number of 50's and 60's electrics that have firmly established themselves as collectible. Most players and prospective collectors also know that old Martins are extremely desirable and probably always will be. But, to identify a list of collectible guitars that will withstand the test of time is perhaps premature and certainly beyond the scope of this presentation.

Most guitars that are presently collectible conform to the generally accepted beliefs that the best acoustic instruments were made before World War II and the most desirable electrics were made before the greatly increased demand (and subsequent reduction in quality) after the mid-sixties. In recent years, many manufacturers are again producing acoustic and electric guitars of excellent quality. This occurrence has, to some degree, actually been generated by the interest in older guitars. Some of these recent guitars may include a number of future collectibles.

For the present, though, a collectible guitar would be defined as one that is out of production. Often the most desirable piece is the original or earlier version of a guitar that is currently being produced. Such is the case with many of the most famous guitars. Martin Dreadnoughts, Fender Telecasters and Stratocasters, and Gibson Les Paul Standards are all available as new instruments at present with nearly identical specifications as the originals. From a utility standpoint, these guitars would compare quite favorably with their namesakes, but from a collector's standpoint there is no comparison. The old guitars possess historic and artistic value that is recreated but not contained in the reissues. The classics have earned their place in guitar history due to the unity of art, technology, and craftsmanship represented in the most perfect examples of form following function.

What to Collect

Most importantly, a person should collect what he or she likes! Your collecting activities should be a natural extension of your guitar playing interests. As later chapters will detail, most collectors began their collection by searching for a specific instrument. As a general rule of thumb, stick with what you know about, as you will learn there is a great deal to know and a lack of knowledge can be very costly.

Collecting is a developmental process, and a person has no choice but to start where he or she is and progress from there gradually. For example, if you now own an older guitar, begin by learning all you can about that specific instrument. Then you may wish to explore the guitar's origins by locating an older version or the original after which it was patterned. Many collectors have assembled a nice group of guitars by such a modest process.

This may be a good time to attempt a clarification of the term "collector" as its current use leads to potential misunderstanding. The traditional definition of a collector refers to an individual who assembles a group of related items with a specific historical or thematic reference. Many guitar players actively seek and "collect" a number of guitars. Some of these players may also be part time or big time dealers. One individual could conceivably be a collector, a dealer, and a player. Such a circumstance is actually not unusual. At present, there appears to be only a limited, but growing, group of individuals who are primarily concerned with collecting rather than playing or dealing. By the nature of the item being collected, the classification of guitar enthusiasts will remain imprecise. Coin collectors or stamp collectors do not spend or lick their collectibles, but guitar collectors definitely do play their guitars. Guitar collectors will assert that the utility value of the instrument makes it the perfect collectible. The ability to hold and manipulate your investment in such intimate circumstances as the artistic and therapeutic expression of music is a compelling situation. This experience is further enhanced by the fact that the collectible guitars are of the finest quality and provide a sense of identity and continuity in the life of the collector. The reality that the collectors' guitars are still highly desirable as professional instruments further complicates the collector/player dichotomy. The majority of professional guitarists own a vintage guitar or two; some have acquired extensive collections. Are these individuals collectors or players? Some of these guitarists are obviously both, but it may be more constructive to attempt a classification scheme of the old guitars themselves.

The classification of specific instruments as "vintage guitars" is a difficult, subjective, and evolving process. As previously mentioned, this guide will not attempt such a task. But, given a specific example of an accepted vintage guitar, the instrument can be roughly designated as a "player's guitar" or a "collector's guitar." This differentiation refers to the degree of originality and condition of the instrument. For example, a refinished 1961 Fender Stratocaster with new frets and tuners is an excellent player's guitar with great utility value, but definitely not a collector's piece. The value of this guitar would also be less than half that of a completely original example. Therefore, it is obvious that the collector would seek only instruments in as original condition as possible. This last statement will be elaborated as a primary theme of this guide.

Fun or Profit

Can't a person experience personal satisfaction as well as make a profit with his or her guitar collection? Well, yes, but it is safer to focus on the fun aspect. Many individuals have certainly profited financially from their guitar collecting activities, but to do so is not as easy as it once was. Musicians, as well as the general public, are well aware of the fact that the prices for select old guitars have risen dramatically over the last ten years or so. More often than not, the inexperienced guitar seller actually thinks his or her instrument is worth a lot more than its market value. Even if a little old lady was willing to sell you her deceased husband's old guitar (an early Fender Telecaster in mint condition, let's say) for two hundred dollars, would it be fair not to inform her of its real value? Similar ethical dilemmas can still be encountered these days, but its likelihood is so remote as to relegate such to a merely academic debate.

The vintage guitar market is still dominated by musicians and, therefore, the market is not entirely stable due to fads and changes in musical styles. The vintage guitars that demand the most money are still completely compatible with popular music. It remains to be seen whether an instrument that becomes undesirable from a contemporary musical standpoint will maintain its collector's value. Of course, there are many indicators that the vintage market is strong and still maturing. The traditional group of art and antique collectors including doctors, lawyers, bankers and wealthy industrialists are becoming more in evidence within the guitar collecting community. Keep in mind that most of the aforementioned group are also players from the guitar generation that now have surplus income. Investment potential is likely not their only motive, but their presence and serious collecting activities lend some potential stability to the market. The vintage instrument market is also an international market, further strengthening the demand for quality guitars. The Japanese have been especially active due to their fascination with American music and pop culture of the 50's and 60's, as well as their available capital, and genuine respect for the instruments.

There are likely much safer investments than vintage guitars, but collectors can take some precautions with respect to their purchases which should safeguard their investments. It is wise to stick to the most accepted collector's guitars and not buy altered instruments. In other words, don't count on a "player's guitar" increasing in value, but a genuine collector's piece should increase over time like fine art. Some would argue that guitars are neither art nor craft because of their mass-produced machine-made origins, and therefore not comparable to a Picasso or a Stradivarius. But, such an opinion is based on a limited perspective and a constricted view of the classification of art objects.

It can be argued that the manufacturing of the most desirable acoustic guitars involved a great deal of craftsmanship. While the production of the mid-century electrics relied heavily on precision machinery, that fact hardly disqualifies them as art objects. Frank Lloyd Wright, the American architect, first spoke of the machine as an artist's tool in the late 1800's. Over the years and through various schools and movements in art and design the concept of "design as art" has been clearly established. Thus, the classic electric and acoustic guitars are worthy of our admiration from the long-standing twentieth century design ideal of striving for the most perfect "unity of art and technology" (the Bauhaus motto).

Certain "classic" examples of mass-produced consumer goods have truly achieved the status of museum quality works. These select objects will retain their value for future generations, while the imitative, cheap, and frankly bizarre items may retain only a passing curiosity as nostalgic icons of popular culture.

The baby boomers will continue to collect guitars for the next twenty years or more. These guitars from their youth have great nostalgic appeal whether they are Telecasters or Teisco's. The question for collectors with longer term investment interests is: Which guitars will still be coveted by the children of the boomers? The safe money will stick with the "classics" and pass on the Jetson's lunchboxes of the guitar world.

Mid and Late 50's Les Paul Juniors & Specials. One of each in single cutaway and double cutaway. All in TV "Limed mahogany finish"

Collector Tim Matyas first saw this early 50's Fender Telecaster being played by a local musician when he was just a kid. He eventually ended up with it.

Les Paul Standards with PAF humbucking pickups - one in sunburst with curley maple and one gold top

Standing Room Only

All photos this page courtesy of Tim Matyas

11

WHY DO WE GO NUTS FOR VINTAGE GUITARS?

(Guitar Collector Survey, Report 1)

What is this mania for old guitars? Excessive and unreasonable enthusiasm abounds in activities connected with vintage instruments. Some consider this intense involvement to be an obsession, a fever, and even a sickness. Could this underinvestigated, unnamed syndrome actually be a psychiatric disorder? Of course not, at least I don't think so.

Once contracted, this interest in old guitars may be terminal. My own symptoms have increased rather than diminished over the years: I can no longer hear or look at the number 59 without thinking about a sunburst Les Paul, I am compelled to purchase tradin' type newspapers in every city I visit, I have taken my old Strat apart for the eighth time excavating for new discoveries, and I have trouble sleeping when anything that is pre-CBS or has PAF's is for sale nearby. If you recognize any of these symptoms, you too may be experiencing some form of this old guitar mania.

So what is this craze all about, and in what forms does it manifest itself? Well, I'm not sure, but I intend to find out. The psychological literature and available academic studies provide clues, but no definitive answers. More data is needed. A questionnaire was developed and a survey of guitar collectors has begun. It seemed reasonable to begin with collectors, as this is an obvious form of the mania, but not all individuals interested in vintage guitars would consider themselves collectors. The primary research question is: Why do we go nuts for vintage guitars?

This is not a simple question to answer. The psychological issues and personality dimensions involved are complex. A psychologist's answer to this question would be dependent on his or her particular theoretical reference. In other words, your guess is as good as mine. Actually, academic psychology does not spend a great deal of time wondering about guitar collectors.

For fun, though, let me present some very brief, theoretical positions as they would relate to the question: Why do we go nuts for vintage guitars? Psychoanalytic (Freudian) theorists would have a field day with collectors of any type and individuals that "love" guitars. Freud was concerned with unconscious motives and conflicts that manifest themselves as psychiatric symptoms. These unconscious conflicts often relate to sexual themes. To love a guitar is to attach some symbolic sexual significance to the object. The nature and origin of the significance would be different for each individual and unavailable to consciousness. So, according to this point of view, we would not know why we "go nuts" for vintage guitars. Sounds a little weird, I know, but there are some real sexual associations with guitars. Was Jimi's Strat a female he made love to and directed aggression towards (another important Freudian drive), or was it an extension of his male anatomy? All of the above, it would appear.

As far as collectors go, Freud would have some even stranger seeming notions. Freud conceived of development as taking place in stages centered around the three vital organ systems of orality, anality and genitality. Freud would view collectors as "anal characters." The anal stage involves the dominance of the anal-eliminative system, and personality development takes place with respect to toilet training. A person could conceivably be "fixated" at the anal stage because of overly harsh or overly indulgent parental approaches to toilet training. The accumulation of possessions is connected to "anal eroticism" which relates to sexual pleasure associated with earlier experiences of holding back bowel functioning. Sounds kind of sickening, doesn't it? Some individuals do possess the traits of "anal characters," but how they got that way may have nothing to do with toilet training.

A more down-to-earth approach to the question about vintage guitars would be represented by a group of theories which have been referred to as environmental-learning or behavioral. These theories are more concerned with behavior than mental events (thoughts and feelings). From this point of view, we learned to like or dislike old guitars through our own experiences. The processes of conditioning and reinforcement are central. You have heard of Ivan Pavlov and his dogs. A simple kind of conditioning is Jimi Hendrix - ding - Stratocaster. If our experiences and associations with old guitars have been positive and rewarding we are more likely to favor them.

While sympathetic with behavioral theories, I prefer to employ more cognitive (conscious mental events) aspects to deal with the issue of vintage guitar mania. Specifically, the construct of "ego involvement" is appealing. "Ego," in this context, refers to "self" or the individual as aware of himself or herself. This can be quite an involved and complicated process to discuss, but in essence I am concerned with the concepts of identity and self worth. An object that we have some ego-involvement with is one that is important to us in terms of who we are. Clothes are an obvious example of this. Some styles fit the image we have of ourselves, and other styles we would not be "caught dead in." A person's guitar can be an extremely personal extension of self, and thus ego-involvement is an issue. Discussions about personal preferences for guitars are often emotionally charged for this reason. Seldom are players' opinions neutral on the issue of old guitars; for example, some love them, others seem to hate them.

I am interested in how others have involved their egos and identities with vintage guitars and why they "go nuts" for them. Just as individual identities are unique, each person's interests in old guitars will

The Dean of the American Vintage Guitar Scene.
George Gruhn in the showroom of his Nashville Shop.

likely vary considerably. I suspect, though, that there will be commonalities and we can learn something about ourselves by knowing more about other vintage guitar buffs and collectors. The rare guitars have been written about in detail, but what do we know about the rare personalities in this field?

The first two respondents to participate in the "Guitar Collector Survey" are George Gruhn and James Werner. George Gruhn is well known as an authority on vintage guitars from his writings on the subject, and as a dealer of fine vintage instruments. James Werner is known to all "Fender freaks" for his continued documentation of Fender serial numbers, and large Fender collection.

Below are excerpts from the responses of Gruhn and Werner on selected Guitar Collector Survey (GCS) questions:

GCS: How many years have you collected guitars?

Gruhn: I have collected guitars since 1963.

Werner: In actual practice, since late 1966 - early 1967; in thought, since mid-to late 1962.

GCS: How many guitars are in your personal collection?

Gruhn: I do not personally collect at present. I have one banjo, one viola, and one mandolin, but all other pieces are basically dealing stock.

Werner: As of 6/22/84, 58 basses, guitars and lap steels.

GCS: What kind of guitars do you collect, and why?

Gruhn: When I did collect guitars for my personal collection, it was because I personally liked them. I collected pieces which I considered to be of great historic and aesthetic merit. I was interested only in pieces that were fully original. I especially favor model 45 Martins, and Loar signed Gibson L-5's.

Werner: Fender (does anyone else make guitars?) as a brand name, solid body as a type. I collect basses, guitars, lap steels and mandolins as models, any of these in Pre-CBS (before January '65 in construction) and some post-CBS (after December '64 in construction) based on certain features: discontinued models, limited editions and rarity of model, etc. I collect because it relaxes me (sometimes), it's interesting and fun to talk to new people about a common interest. I don't do it as a status/money symbol.

GCS: What is your personal definition of a "guitar collector"? (How many instruments, vintage vs. utility, etc.)

Gruhn: I would say that it is not so much a function of how many instruments one has. Certainly, utility instruments are not what I consider to be the definition of a collection. A collector must have items of high quality and historical merit. The pieces must have some relation to each other, for example: a complete series of all types of D-28's ever made, or perhaps all styles of 45 Martins' ever made. Having a group of instruments for utility purposes such as some rock and roll players may have (20 reworked Stratocasters, for instance) is not a collection. A plumber with a tool chest full of wrenches is not a wrench collector.

Werner: I see a guitar collector as anyone involved (theory or practice) in getting and maintaining guitars by having them in stock working order. A collector to me is a person who collects knowledge and information to know the who, what, where, when and why of a guitar as compared to other guitars, and upgrading within the collection to obtain the best possible example of a specific model(s). The "number of instruments" has nothing to do with anything, and "vintage vs. utility" sounds more like "status collecting" as opposed to "working collection."

GCS: In your opinion, what do you see to be the primary motivating force behind personal guitar collections (small or large collections)? If other than financial, please describe psychological or emotional factors.

Gruhn: The motivating force behind a guitar collection I see to be the same as behind any collection of historical artifacts. If you dig deeply enough into the reasons why anyone collects anything, you will only uncover a bunch of neuroses.

Werner: Collectors are interested in obtaining rare vintage, collectible guitars to play, look at, sell-trade for other guitars. The chance to deal with famous collectors/players is a factor, and being able to make money with their hobby — that is how I define most other collectors.

I prefer to correspond with collectors who can answer (and ask) questions, share knowledge, and talk about their collection. I am interested in: what they have, what they want, others in the field they know, stories about how they got something, confirmation/reinforcement/ disproving of knowledge, where their collection is going, etc. I call it having a good attitude. Stories about the one that got away and the one that didn't get away are also interesting.

Gruhn and Werner responded to various other questions on the GCS. George Gruhn's favorite guitars are model 45 Martins and Lloyd Loar signed Gibson L-5's. "The 45 Martins that I personally like the best are those made between '34 and '38; Loar L-5's are 1923 and 1924. These instruments are special to me because they are the absolute ultimate examples of the maker's craft." Jim Werner's favorite guitar is a Telecaster (March, 1960). It belonged to his friend, Joe McClean, who initially got him interested in collecting. In reference to the Telecaster, Jim states: "It feels great and sounds very nice. I think of all the dozens of hours of music that Joe and previous owners put through it." Another favorite guitar of Werner's is his 1950 Broadcaster, " 'cause it's one of the first and rather limited."

Gruhn and Werner were asked to rate the significance of eight "important elements" of vintage guitars listed below:

_____ appearance
_____ feel
_____ sound
_____ craftsmanship
_____ historical significance
_____ association with a famous player
_____ exclusivity, status appeal
_____ investment potential

"Craftsmanship" and "historical significance" were rated the two most important elements by both Gruhn and Werner. "Association with a famous player" was not considered personally important to either of them. Gruhn states: "Association with a famous player is totally irrelevant to me, though it is of some significance to some collectors." Jim Werner feels similarly. His 1960 Telecaster was once played by Jeff Beck, which he mentioned reluctantly. He is not interested in what he calls "stars' guitars" or "stars' guitars-itis." Werner states: "The Tele means more to me that Joe McClean had it than anyone else that may have played it. The only time I mention Beck or a chance to sell to Entwhistle is if I'm asked. It's flattering, but not why I collect."

George Gruhn considers the money-related items (exclusivity, investment potential) as important for obvious business reasons. On the "exclusivity" element he comments: "Exclusivity and status appeal are important, but so far as I'm concerned, there are many pieces which are sleepers and I'm much more interested in my own opinion of a piece rather than what others have to say about it." Werner is especially negative about the money-related items. He states: "You've probably noted I've downgraded all the money style questions — here's why: I'm not independently wealthy. I work for a living, have certain basic needs to care for and like to acquire certain 'non-essential-for-living items.' I know roughly what I'm willing to pay for something (based on what it's worth to me — not what anybody says it's worth)." Investment potential is not important to Werner because he does not plan on selling his collection.

As most children collect something at some point in their development, I was interested in Gruhn and Werner in terms of children's collections. They both collected things as children. Gruhn collected animals, particularly snakes and turtles. He states: "I started collecting snakes when I was eight years old. I began with beasts in general when I was about four; I began with bugs and worked up. George further commented: "at this point [I] could truthfully say that I know as much about snakes as I do about guitars." Werner collected: "dinosaurs (figures, models) and knowledge about them, rocks, coins, Tarzan comic books and baseball cards."

So, can we answer the question about why we go nuts for vintage guitars from the comments of these two important collectors? Well, probably not, but it's a start. There are a number of similarities in their comments, and significant differences. They agree on the most important "elements" of vintage guitars. They both have inquisitive minds and sought knowledge about things that interested them (snakes and dinosaurs to guitars). Gruhn once had a "large personal collection" and many pieces were not for sale. There could be a progression or stages of development that collectors go through.

They differ on the "vintage is better" issue. Gruhn states: "I think that I and others prefer vintage instruments because they are the best. They look the best, they sound the best, they feel the best, they have the most historic interest, and those that are truly well-constructed have 'soul.'" The reader should keep in mind that Gruhn is specifically referring to acoustic instruments such as the Lloyd Loar signed Gibsons and pre-World War II-style Martins, I believe. On the subject of vintage superiority, Werner states: "'Vintage is better' — I don't say this. I prefer 'used' or sometimes 'old.' Different can be shown/proven, 'better' is more of a personal preference."

George Gruhn's interest in collecting guitars began as a "hobby that got out of hand." He has turned that hobby into a successful business, and we have all benefitted from reading his articles. George appears to be more rational than emotional about vintage guitars at this point, as they are his business, but his identity to us, and I suspect to himself, remains associated with vintage instruments.

In the early sixties Jim Werner became interested in guitars. He states: "The Beach Boys became popular and turned my head around about music. I found out the Beach Boys played 'Fenders' (aren't they part of a car?) and wanted the models like they played." Jim plays bass and guitar but does not consider himself much of a musician; "I realized I didn't have the talent to play, but I did have the talent to collect!"

The most intriguing aspect of Jim Werner's interest in Fenders could be called "collecting as a social activity." Jim is a modest and sincere guy that enjoys keeping in touch with collectors all over the world. He describes himself as having been a withdrawn child, and collecting has apparently been a vehicle to his social development. Collecting is also an important aspect of his identity as THE "Fender Collector." His self-satisfaction does not come from being an expert on the subject of Fender musical instruments. He says: "I'm no expert — I know experts," and "I know very little and I'm able to prove it." The self-satisfaction involved in a social sense is related to helping others locate guitars, disseminating information freely, and generally furthering the state of knowledge on Fenders.

I plan to continue this project, in fact, I am just getting started. Why do you go nuts for vintage guitars? I'd really like to know. Don't be surprised if you receive a survey in the mail one of these days. More "case reports" of collectors and vintage guitar owners are needed to better understand this mania. Who knows, a "cure" may even be discovered, if anyone wants one.

50's Les Paul, Jr's and Special. Two Sunburst and two "TV's".

Late 50's Gibson Les Paul models: 3/4 Jr.; Jr.; Special in Cherry finish and TV finish and EBO bass.

Gibson Les Paul Standards, original series (1952-1960). Note development of features through the years.

Flock of Firebirds & Thunderbirds

A Rack of Rick's

All guitars this page courtesy of Brian Fischer Collection

Telecasters & Esquire

Custom Color Strats - not fun in black and white.

Fender Musiclander/ Swinger's in red, blue, green and black

All guitars this page courtesy of Brian Fischer Collection

BUILDING A COLLECTION

Gathering Knowledge

The importance of historical as well as up-to-the minute knowledge on the vintage market cannot be overstated. Prices on specific guitars will rise and fall over time. Sometimes dramatic gains or losses can occur over a relatively short period of time on individual instruments. A good example of this involved the case of "Stratmania" during the late 1980's. The prices for pre-CBS Fender Stratocasters more than doubled over the period of a year or so, topped off, and then fell off considerably. Buying an old Strat during that period was a tricky business. On the other hand, many older guitars do not seem to gain or lose value over a relatively long period of time, while some other instruments continue to gain steadily, abeit gradually, over time.

Most collectors read and usually subscribe to the leading guitar magazines (Guitar Player and Guitar World). Both publications keep up with the vintage guitar market and are invaluable as a source of current information on vintage guitars and market trends. Pay specific attention to Richard Smith's "Rare Bird" column and his other articles on guitars and collecting. Any past or present article written by George Gruhn is definitely required reading. After you have purchased a guitar magazine, the next step is to turn to the last pages and subscribe to every dealer's list available. The price of the subscription is nominal, and the regular evaluating of these lists amounts to the best market index of vintage guitar prices. You will notice that prices differ somewhat depending on location, but definite going rates and trends can be evidenced. Gruhn Guitar's list from Nashville is very comprehensive and a good place to start. Other valuable sources of information are guitar collector periodicals such as the Guitar Digest, 20th Century Guitar, and Vintage Guitar, which contain articles on guitars and collecting as well as instruments for sale by private owners.

Upon studying these dealer's lists, you will notice that many of the most valuable pieces seldom appear on them. This is due to a number of factors. Most dealers maintain "want files" and develop relationships with their best clientele. Therefore, when highly desired guitars are sold by a dealer they do not always show up on their list. Many collectors sell directly to other collectors and the transactions do not become public. This situation is not as discouraging as it may seem. The next step to acquiring knowledge on the vintage market is to develop relationships with other collectors and guitar enthusiasts. Most collectors and dealers are glad to share information. The most famous "unknown" collector, James Werner, has made a life of being accessible to collectors and maintaining a genuinely altruistic standard for the collecting community. Collecting is also a social activity and a good deal of a person's enjoyment is derived from the friendships developed and stories shared.

Guitar Identification

The heading for this section is borrowed from André Duchossoir's book of the same name. This publication contains essential information for the aspiring collector on dating the guitars made by Fender, Gibson, Gretsch and Martin. It is necessary for the guitar enthusiast to be able to date the instrument (sometimes approximate) and be able to appraise its originality by a thorough understanding of the structural details of a specific make and model. Such matters can present many challenges, but correct identification is critical. The specific year of a guitar's manufacture is, of course, an essential element in the determination of its value. Sometimes the exact year is important such as the first year of a guitar's manufacture, but more often it is a specific model that is desired as identified by its unique features. In such a case, the features can span a two or three year period. In any event, the year is still important, but a more difficult aspect to evaluate

Registration opens February 3 at 10:00am

Genealogy   Adults   Older Adults   English

Hidden Treasures: Courthouse Records for Family History

Tuesday, March 18, 6:00pm–7:30pm
Plain Community Branch

Registration opens February 3 at 10:00am

Continuing Education   Culture   Genealogy   History   Adults   +1 more

Get It Together!

Thursday, March 20, 2:00pm–3:00pm
Jackson Community Branch

Registration opens February 3 at 10:00am

Continuing Education   Genealogy   Adults   Older Adults   English

Hidden Treasures: Courthouse Records for Family History

Monday, April 07, 3:30pm–5:00pm
East Canton Branch

Registration opens March 3 at 10:00am

Continuing Education   Genealogy   History   Adults   Older Adults

How to Plan the Best Family Reunion

Tuesday, April 08, 6:00pm–7:30pm
Plain Community Branch

Registration opens March 3 at 10:00am

Continuing Education   Culture   Genealogy   Recreation   Adults   +1 more

Local History & Genealogy Fair

Saturday, May 03, 11:00am–3:00pm
Main Library

Genealogy   History   Adults   Older Adults   English

Journaling My Story

Wednesday, May 21, 2:00pm–3:30pm
DeHoff Memorial Branch

Registration opens April 1 at 10:00am

Genealogy   Writing   Adults   Older Adults   English

Hidden Treasures: Courthouse Records for Family History

Thursday, May 22, 2:00pm–3:30pm
Jackson Community Branch

Registration opens April 1 at 10:00am

Beginning Scrapbooking Workshop

Tuesday, January 14, 6:00pm-7:00pm
Plain Community Branch

Registration required (9 spots remaining) Register for event

Continuing Education   Crafts   Genealogy   Adults   Older Adults

Genealogy Databases @ Stark Library

Wednesday, January 15, 2:00pm-3:30pm
DeHoff Memorial Branch

Registration required (18 spots remaining) Register for event

Continuing Education   Genealogy   Technology   Adults   Older Adults

Accessing Historical Newspapers

Tuesday, January 21, 3:30pm-5:00pm
East Canton Branch

Registration required (10 spots remaining) Register for event

Continuing Education   Genealogy   History   Adults   Older Adults

Effectively Using the Federal Census

Monday, February 03, 3:30pm-5:00pm
East Canton Branch

Registration required (20 spots remaining) Register for event

Continuing Education   Genealogy   History   Adults   Older Adults

Beginning Genealogy

Wednesday, February 19, 2:00pm-3:30pm
DeHoff Memorial Branch

Registration required (23 spots remaining) Register for event

Genealogy   Adults   Older Adults   English

AI Insights: Demystifying Artificial Intelligence

Wednesday, March 12, 10:00am-11:00am
DeHoff Memorial Branch

Registration opens February 3 at 10:00am

Genealogy   Adults   Older Adults   English

From Branches to Roots: Exploring Your Family History

Thursday, March 13, 6:00pm-7:30pm
Main Library

Registration opens February 3 at 10:00am

Genealogy   Adults   Older Adults   English

Hidden Treasures: Courthouse Records for Family History

Tuesday, March 18, 6:00pm-7:30pm
Plain Community Branch

Registration opens February 3 at 10:00am

Continuing Education   Culture   Genealogy   History   Adults   +1 more

Get It Together!

Thursday, March 20, 2:00pm-3:00pm
Jackson Community Branch

Registration opens February 3 at 10:00am

Continuing Education   Genealogy   Adults   Older Adults   English

Hidden Treasures: Courthouse Records for Family History

Monday, April 07, 3:30pm-5:00pm
East Canton Branch

Registration opens March 3 at 10:00am

Continuing Education   Genealogy   History   Adults   Older Adults

How to Plan the Best Family Reunion

Tuesday, April 08, 6:00pm-7:30pm
Plain Community Branch

Registration opens March 3 at 10:00am

Continuing Education   Culture   Genealogy   Recreation   Adults   +1 more

Local History & Genealogy Fair

Saturday, May 03, 11:00am-3:00pm
Main Library

Genealogy   History   Adults   Older Adults   English

Journaling My Story

Wednesday, May 21, 2:00pm-3:30pm
DeHoff Memorial Branch

Registration opens April 1 at 10:00am

Genealogy   Writing   Adults   Older Adults   English

Hidden Treasures: Courthouse Records for Family History

Thursday, May 22, 2:00pm-3:30pm
Jackson Community Branch

Registration opens April 1 at 10:00am

Beginning Scrapbooking Workshop

Tuesday, January 14, 6:00pm–7:00pm
Plain Community Branch

Registration required (9 spots remaining) Register for event

Continuing Education   Crafts   Genealogy   Adults   Older Adults

Genealogy Databases @ Stark Library

Wednesday, January 15, 2:00pm–3:30pm
DeHoff Memorial Branch

Registration required (18 spots remaining) Register for event

Continuing Education   Genealogy   Technology   Adults   Older Adults

Accessing Historical Newspapers

Tuesday, January 21, 3:30pm–5:00pm
East Canton Branch

Registration required (10 spots remaining) Register for event

Continuing Education   Genealogy   History   Adults   Older Adults

Effectively Using the Federal Census

Monday, February 03, 3:30pm–5:00pm
East Canton Branch

Registration required (20 spots remaining) Register for event

Continuing Education   Genealogy   History   Adults   Older Adults

Beginning Genealogy

Wednesday, February 19, 2:00pm–3:30pm
DeHoff Memorial Branch

Registration required (23 spots remaining) Register for event

Genealogy   Adults   Older Adults   English

AI Insights: Demystifying Artificial Intelligence

Wednesday, March 12, 10:00am–11:00am
DeHoff Memorial Branch

Registration opens February 3 at 10:00am

Genealogy   Adults   Older Adults   English

From Branches to Roots: Exploring Your Family History

Thursday, March 13, 6:00pm–7:30pm
Main Library

concerns the guitar's condition and whether or not it has been altered in any way. Certain alterations, as has been discussed, can render the instrument completely undesirable to the collector.

Unethical sellers may misrepresent an instrument or, more commonly, the seller is simply misinformed (but may act quite sure of himself nevertheless). In any event the buyer must be armed with a great deal of information and direct experience. Unfortunately, a good degree of first hand experience and direct contact with the instrument is necessary. Detailed photographs are extremely valuable and fortunately are now readily available in a number of publications, but they are not a substitute for actual physical contact. To be able to identify the originality of finishes and details such as frets and small parts requires more intimate experience than pictures can provide. Many collectors have learned these lessons, sometimes the hard way, by owning a good number of instruments. A less expensive, but clearly not as informative, approach is to attend guitar shows. Attendance at such events also provides excellent opportunities to meet guitar enthusiasts and dealers from all over the country. Most regions throughout the United States now feature yearly guitar shows, which is a welcome development as not all guitar collectors live in Texas. If possible, though, check out one of the big Texas shows to really get a feel for the enormity of the vintage guitar enterprise.

The potential player in the vintage guitar market will need much more information than is contained in Guitar Identification. Fortunately, Monsieur Duchossoir, as well as others, have provided a number of excellent reference books on vintage guitars, most notably American Guitars by Tom Wheeler, Gibson Electrics and The Fender Stratocaster by A. R. Duchossoir, Rickenbacker by Richard R. Smith, Martin Guitars — A History by Mike Longworth and The Guitars of Friedrich Gretsch by Jay Scott. A complete study of these publications is necessary to be knowledgeable about the guitars that comprise the vintage market.

These books are actually very exciting themselves, not as great as an early Fender color catalogue, mind you, but really impressive. The authors, all dedicated experts, have provided guitar enthusiasts with an incredible degree of detail through their extensive research, and detail is the name of the game in the collecting business. Please refer to the bibliography at the end of this book for information on these works and other important references for collectors.

Where to Look

Where should a person look for a vintage guitar? Everywhere! The search for a specific instrument can be aggravating, but also enjoyable and worth the effort. The survey participants were queried as to their preferred methods of locating old guitars, and a variety of approaches were shared. Many individuals preferred to buy from individuals (especially original owners) rather than dealers. Some collectors enjoy a search of pawn shows, flea markets and garage sales. Other individuals have advertised in national publications, and some have even posted notices in retirement homes. Music stores and the classified ads of city newspapers as well as smaller tradin' types of papers are also obvious potential sources.

The frustrating truth is that it has become increasingly difficult to locate collector's guitars through the classifieds, yard sales and the like. But, don't let the level of difficulty dissuade you from the search, as it is still possible to come up with some great finds. To locate altered or "player's guitars" through this method is a lot easier. Again, a person will need to be well informed when doing business with amateur dealers or sellers of used guitars. Most experienced collectors can recall amazing, but ultimately humorous, stories of private sellers marketing 1949 Les Pauls, pre-CBS Stratocasters (circa 1975), $15,000 Les Paul Jr.'s and the like.

When going to view the instrument at an individual's house it is a good idea to take cash and a copy of Guitar Identification. With the book you can verify the date and other aspects of the instrument in a calm rational fashion (debates become unnecessary - - "My Dad bought this guitar new in 1957"). Also, be sure to play the guitar (if electric) through an amp to check out the electronics, and don't be afraid to offer less than the asking price. While this method may not net many collector's items, it is a great way to buy utility instruments at often much less than a dealer would have to realize.

The most direct way to obtain a true collectible is to locate the instrument on a dealer's list and call about it. Don't be afraid to ask detailed questions about the guitar's condition, degree of originality, etc. Most dealers, for a dollar or two, will gladly send you a picture of the guitar. You may lose it if you hesitate, though, as the most desirable instruments are usually sold first, sometimes before the list even reaches your home. Most, if not all, dealers will give you at least 24 hours after you receive the guitar to check it out. If the instrument does not meet your approval, you will need to call the dealer to get a return authorization to ship the guitar back to them. The guitar should be shipped (most often by United Parcel Service) in the same container it arrived in. You will likely be responsible for the return shipping. Don't let this deter you from sending the guitar back if it does not meet your **complete** approval. This method of conducting business with the large scale dealers is relatively safe and reasonable. Many novice guitar collectors are apprehensive about buying from the big dealers, but most of their fears are unfounded. You will be required to pay the going market rate for the instrument, but this is often necessary.

Another logical way to buy a vintage guitar is to attend one of the many

Steve Melkisethian at his booth. Mid '80's. Dallas Guitar Show with his favorite (non-Fender) guitar - a '61 Gretsch Silver Jet.

Guitar Digest Publishers and Sponsors of Ohio Guitar Show.
L to R - Marc Newman, Marc Wayner & Stephen Hopkins.
1990 Summer Ohio Guitar Show

guitar shows. The vintage guitar periodicals as well as the major guitar magazines regularly publish notices as to the scheduled shows around the country. There are advantages as well as drawbacks to purchasing a guitar in this fashion. A definite plus (as opposed to buying from a stock list) is being able to inspect the instrument in person. Again, don't be shy about asking detailed questions and negotiating the price. The down side of buying at a show is that you will not have a leisurely number of hours to determine your final purchase (approval) of the instrument. In fact, the often fast paced and crowded environment of the shows tends to encourage a more impulsive decision. The trick is to know the market, know the instruments and know what you are looking for, which is quite a trick!

The most desirable collector's guitars are usually sold or traded from dealer to dealer or collector to collector. Anyone can participate in this process, though, by meeting others in the field and letting them know what you are looking for. This does not represent bargain basement shopping, but at this upper level other considerations can take precedence over price.

What to Buy

What to buy is, of course, a subjective matter. This guide is intended for the individual that wishes to get started or further his or her private collection. It is wise to let speculating to the professionals and stick with the guitars you like and wish to keep. It is very possible to buy and sell guitars to further your personal collection, but making enough of a profit to offset the effort takes experience. The situation with selling or trading guitars can be compared to the car market with respect to the concepts of wholesale and retail values (with the exception that the values will likely be more variable and arbitrary). When a transaction involves trading or selling to a dealer, the seller will be offered wholesale prices. To realize the current retail value of an instrument, the owner will need to market it independently. It can be a challenge to market a vintage guitar yourself, but don't let that stop you from trying. Another alternative to independent marketing of the instrument involves the practice of selling the piece on consignment to a dealer. The practices and policies for such arrangements differ from dealer to dealer, but essentially result in the instrument being marketed and sold at retail by the dealer and the dealer retaining a percentage for his or her services. The sale of an instrument by this method will take some time, but will likely net the owner more than the wholesale value. The business of selling is, or course, more involved than this summary and deserving of its own book length treatment.

The conservative advice offered by this guide is to collect what you like, but if you wish to preserve your investment, it is safest to accumulate only established collector's guitars in the best condition as possible. The condition of the guitar is of the utmost concern with respect to the high end items, whereas the condition of a "player's guitar" or utility instrument is not as critical with regards to its present or future value. Most dealers describe the condition of their inventory by a simple code:

> **Mint** — Like new, as in freshly minted. This refers to a guitar in absolutely perfect original condition. Such instruments do exist, but they are exceedingly rare and worth disproportionately more than the same model in very good or even excellent condition.

> **Near Mint (NM)** — Like the above, but with very minor wear that is usually not readily observable.

> **Excellent (Ex)** — Can also be graded Ex+ and Ex-. A guitar in excellent condition. Looks extremely good with only minor deficits (minor finish wear, dings or chips, slight plating wear, etc).

> **Very Good (VG)** — Is usually graded VG+ and VG-. This is the most often encountered category of guitar descriptions and ranges from looking pretty good but with very obvious wear and tear to pretty bad with considerable cosmetic deterioration.

> **Good (G)** — This category refers to an instrument that is in stable structural and electrical condition but is in poor cosmetic condition, not to be considered a collectible item unless the instrument is an extremely rare and highly desirable model. Some vintage models in good condition also make excellent "player's guitars" and can look really cool such as a very worn maple neck Strat.

What about the collecting of the cheap stuff that is becoming popular? This practice is apparently of interest to a number of individuals and this guide does not take the position that such is not a legitimate collection. Some of these guitars, like the Danelectros, may turn out to be very good investments, but to hope for these instruments to appreciate, or even hold their value, as a whole, is likely a risky proposition.

Another risky proposition includes guitars that were played or owned by a famous player. These so called "stars' guitars" are usually not very interesting to the collector. There are a number of reasons for this. The primary one is that most available stars' guitars are not vintage guitars. There are notable exceptions to this generality, and if those examples include written and complementary photographic documentation, then such instruments will indeed be highly valued. But, at present only a limited number of these stars' "crossover" (rock 'n roll memorabilia and vintage guitar) guitars are known to exist. (See Appendix B for an example of such). Most of the guitars owned by the Hard Rock Café, for example, certainly qualify for the memorabilia category, but many are not what would usually be categorized as a vintage guitar. This categorization is, of course, a matter of opinion, but many of the newer guitars that are simply signed by the stars would not be of interest to most collectors.

Some of the most interesting stars' guitars are not so easily classified, a prime example being the Fender Stratocasters of Jimi Hendrix. Hendrix-era Stratocasters (essentially 1966-1970) are desirable as collector's guitars because of his use of the instrument even though they do not conform to the usual pre-CBS standard. However, Jimi's Strats are likely to be most valuable from a rock memorabilia standpoint and command record prices not at a Texas guitar show but at Sotheby's in London.

Mint Condition - 1956. Fender Stratocaster, blonde with gold parts sometimes referred to as a "Mary Kay" Strat.

Tele Thinline 1971 custom color

1957 Gibson Les Paul TV, Jr.

The Da Pra Burst, 1959 #9-0913, Spectacular even in black & white.

Sunburst Curley maple Gibson ES-5 with 3 p.90's (1954)

James Werner - "The Striped Shirt Photo" September 1979
"First Over-Kill credibility shot"

SOMETIMES A GUITAR IS JUST A GUITAR

(Guitar Collector Survey, Report 2.)

In the last report from the Guitar Collector Survey, traditional psychological theories were applied to the question "Why do we go nuts for vintage guitars?" Since that time, "case reports" have been collected on individuals seized with symptomatology characteristic of the "Old Guitar Mania" (OGM). In an attempt to understand what this craze is all about, collectors have been asked how they initially became interested in collecting guitars, why guitar collecting is an important part of their life, and what guitar collecting does for them psychologically.

The responses of the collectors have been categorized into collector-generated theories on the "why we go nuts" question and reveal that OGM exists in various forms and degrees. The first category is the "dream guitar" notion that stems from musician interests and the search for the proper instrument. This search can apparently lead to an "addiction/compulsion" aspect of pursuing guitars. Within the activity of collecting guitars are various psychologically meaningful aspects which have been identified as "recreational/social," "nostalgic appeal," and "personal accomplishment." When reading the comments of the survey respondents, the reader should keep in mind that most of the collectors can identify with all of the aspects presented.

Seldom would a single reason or cause account for a person's interest in old guitars. Multiple factors are always in operation when searching for "causes" of psychological variables.

Vic Da Pra and the author with the "Da Pra" burst - the quintessential Vintage guitar

Dream Guitar

Guitar collectors are guitar players with very few exceptions. Many collectors began their collections by searching for that one special guitar. Vic DaPra of Guitar Gallery in Pennsylvania, a serious player and collector, is a survey participant with an equally serious case of OGM. Vic is known primarily for his collection of "Bursts" and as the owner of the famous Brock/DaPra sunburst Les Paul (featured as the collector's choice in Guitar World September, 1981, and on the jacket of Tom Wheeler's American Guitars).

Vic states, "I became interested in collecting guitars through reading articles on my favorite guitarists at the time. Bloomfield, Page, Beck and Clapton all marvelled at the sound their old Les Pauls had. This aroused my attention enough to try and find one for myself. And to this day, I haven't stopped searching for old guitars." Vic continues the search, most recently for custom color Strats.

Bart Wittrock of Rockin' Robin Guitars in Texas suggests an interesting aspect of the dream guitar theory. Bart asserts, "Music is so personal you need a talisman and guitar players are the worst (best?)." Bart conveys a lot of information in this sentence. Guitarists continue to seek that guitar that has magic power and, as musicians possessing an artistic temperament, they are likely to be quite particular in their choice of an instrument. Bart's favorite guitar is a 1959 Les Paul Standard. When asked why the guitar is so special to him, he responds, "It's magic." - - of course.

Klaus Blasquiz, a musician, journalist, and TV producer from France, collects Fender bass guitars and represents another musician who was searching for his dream guitar, in his case a '62 Fender Jazz Bass.

L to R - The Paga Band - Bernard Paganotti, Bass & Vocals; Bertrand Lajudie, Keyboards; Claude Salmieri, Drums; Klaus Blasquiz, Vocals, Bass & Percussion.

Klaus responds to the question, "Why is guitar collecting an important part of your life?" by stating, "Ask a musician when he finds an instrument he was looking for for years...." Klaus conveys the importance that can be attached to locating that prized axe.

Thomas A. Van Hoose, Ph.D., a clinical psychologist, of all things, is the most recent respondent to the Guitar Collector Survey. Unlike the other psychologist known to this survey (Dr. Bill AKA the Freud of Fender) who collects the "kid stuff" (black face Fender amps and Strats), Dr. Van Hoose collects "serious" jazz guitars. Tom states, "Initially, I became interested in collecting guitars as a by-product of my interest in jazz guitar playing. In college, I bought Jimmy Smith's album featuring Kenny Burrell on guitar, and I became so enamored of his style of guitar playing that I bought several of his records. I then noticed that he played a Gibson Super 400 Guitar, as pictured on some of his record album covers. Several years later, when I became more skilled at playing the guitar, I decided to

Tom Van Hoose playing a '39 Super 400 PN. This was the first year for the cutaway body and the natural finish

get a Super 400 thinking that I could play guitar like Kenny Burrell. After buying a 1967 Super 400 C, I became very interested in it for other reasons such as its craftsmanship, sound, etc. It then seemed to become important to have a second Super 400 that was different from the first one. As they say, the rest is history!" Tom is building a collection of all the standard versions of the Gibson Super 400 Guitar, both acoustic and electric, from 1934 up to the present. He is also writing a book about the Gibson Super 400 Guitar.

Addiction/Compulsion

If an initial stage in guitar collecting is the search for the ultimate personal instrument, or "dream guitar," then the critical stage is the "addiction/compulsion" phase. Somehow in the process of locating the right guitar something happens psychologically and the process becomes as important as the acquisition.

The well known collector and dealer, Norman Harris, of Norman's Rare Guitars in California tells how he initially became interested in collecting guitars, "I was playing in a band and we needed a bass player. We could not find one we were satisfied with so we used two guitar players switching from guitar to bass. I went out and bought an old J Bass (1961) from a newspaper ad for $85.00. I was offered a good profit on the bass and

Norm Harris at his California Shop

Honest Ron Lira in his barn with woodworking machinery, '60 Gibson ES345, 30's Gibson Lap Steel and his first vintage guitar (bought in Oct. '69) a '57 Gibson Les Paul Standard

felt this could be a fun business. My next acquisition was an L-5 C in near mint condition, blond finish. The lady who was selling the guitar was told by her husband to sell everything in the house because they were moving to Japan. (He was already there.) She sold the guitar to me for $20.00. I couldn't believe it! I shook as I handed her the money. I was hooked!" Norm nicely conveys the intensity of emotion that is involved and identifies the addiction analogy. Ron Lira of Honest Ron's Guitars in Oklahoma expresses similar sentiments. Ron states, "I bought my first vintage Les Paul, did some research on it — mostly word-of-mouth — and was hooked on the search and acquisition!" Ron's statement identifies the importance of the "search" process and how it is part of the final acquisition of a piece. Honest Ron, known for his expert repair and restoration work, continues to search for old guitars. He even has a sign on the back of his van that says, "I buy guitars — see driver."

Allan Potter "Montana Al" and Fenders

The search for old guitars may even be more important than the eventual purchase in the "addiction/compulsion" phase of OGM. Allan Potter, a "full time firefighter and full time musician" is a Fender collector who adds insight into the search aspect. "Montana" Al reveals, "It's the high of the hunt, the low of missing and it's like looking for gold — you never know what's in the next pan." "Montana" Al from Everett, Washington has prospected for over 105 Fender instruments to date and hopes to open his own night club and restaurant which will feature the guitars in glass cases on the walls throughout the bar and restaurant (one blond and one sunburst of every model Fender instrument).

Brian Brock, another interesting figure in the guitar world, is also hooked on the search and acquisition of old guitars. Brian does not consider himself a collector per se. He states, "I hedge at the term collect, I mainly accumulate them through the buying and selling process and only have around three that I won't sell." To the question of what guitar collecting does for him, Brian responds, "As a youth it was a great way to torture my parents. As an adult it has evolved into more of a search or quest for a "Lost Icon" or "Maltese Falcon" that you know is just lying in a dusty attic, under a bed, or buried in the back of a hock shop or flea market just waiting to be discovered, nurtured, pampered, played, displayed, and generally brought into your own realm of consciousness. To this day it literally takes me twice as long to travel any distance in a vehicle, as I cannot pass a garage sale or pawn shop."

Brian Brock of Cheyenne, Wyoming, is known as the primary owner of the Brock/DaPra Burst and has elevated the search for old guitars to a "quest." Brian provides more evidence that the search is just as important as the acquisition. "I've pretty much had what I was looking for half a dozen times but always managed to sell it before I realized it couldn't be replaced. As far as what I am currently looking for, I would love to locate the Stratocaster that was stolen from Buddy Holly in the late 50's that is still out there somewhere."

Tom Wittrock of Third Eye Music in Missouri adds a personality dimension to the "addiction/compulsion" notion. Tom says, "Many people feel a need to collect something. It's like a puzzle waiting to be solved. And many people play guitars — for many reasons. When these two ideas are present in one person — a guitar-aholic is a distinct possibility." Tom Wittrock collects Les Paul sunbursts and appears quite hooked, signing his survey with the true addictive admission: "I am a guitar-aholic." Vic DaPra also is aware of the personality aspect that goes along with the "addiction/compulsion." Vic reveals, "I am always looking to expand my collection. I'm the guy you hear about who is always looking for that one a little cleaner or curlier than the one before. I don't think I can have an ultimate goal because as soon as I purchase a piece I'm always looking for a better one."

Individuals who have developed OGM are "addicted" to the search and acquisition.

Tom Wittrock with a few of his curly maple top Les Pauls. L to R - #0-2196, 1960; #9-1228, 1959; #9-0629, 1959; #9-0592, 1959

Bob Reed - Sitting in an English garden with his favorite 1962 Fiesta Red Fender Stratocaster

The high associated with the score appears to be proportional to the time and effort required to locate the piece. The behavior appears to be compulsive, as it is not easy to resist or relinquish. Individuals with perfectionistic/compulsive personalities would seem to be more susceptible, as perfection (complete satisfaction with a piece) is never realized and the tendency to complete a series is ever present. Is OGM a compulsive disorder?

Recreational/Social

An important aspect of guitar collecting is the diversion it can provide from a person's regular business and the social contacts with individuals that share a common interest. Bob Reed, a free lance commercial artist from England, comments on this aspect of collecting. "Guitar collecting is an important part of my life now, as it is a necessary escape from my business life which tends to be somewhat stressful at times. The guitars are a visual reminder of why I put up with the pressures of my working life. My wife maintains I am easier to live with and that I seem to have more purpose in my life." Bob collects Fender electrics and a few British Burns electrics. His favorite guitar is a Fiesta Red Strat (1962). Another European survey respondent is A. R. Duchossoir. André is the French guitar "investigator/historian" who authored several important books on vintage guitars: Gibson Electrics, The Fender Stratocaster and Guitar Identification. André writes, "Guitar collecting used to be a 'world of my own' and I was able (and lucky) to share this wonderful world with a selected few people (especially in France). Later on, it allowed me to meet collectors and addicts from all over the world. What started as a 'solo' venture eventually evolved into a 'passport' to meet people and therefore broadened my scope in every way (guitar-wise and else)." André no longer considers himself a collector! To the question of where his collection is going, André responds, "Nowhere! The trip is over. I've had what I wanted at one time or another. I no longer have that 'collecting fever,' although I still enjoy looking at guitars. During my busy years, my ultimate goal was to own the guitar(s) which would make me the happiest man in the world and end my quest.

A. R. Duchossoir "Back to where it all began... strumming a Broadcaster on what is now Fender Avenue"

To me, guitars are a bit like women; you search for the Holy Grail (whatever it is) and one day it's here within reach and the quest is over. It builds up like a climax and suddenly you realize there is nothing else to look for, but simply to enjoy what you own."

Jeff Ridolfi, a real property appraiser with a public utility firm in San Francisco, comments on why collecting is important. "It is important because it provides a great diversion from my regular daily activities. It's different people, priorities, stories, and fun which provide me with a "break" from the regular....Always a hobby (my only one) — never a business." Jeff has been searching for the ultra rare Pre-CBS custom color, custom Teles and Esquires. Has anyone ever seen one? Tom Van Hoose also discusses this aspect of collecting. "Guitar collecting has become an important part of my life because it fulfills several needs of mine in a very interesting way. First, it is directly associated with music and playing the guitar, both of which I truly enjoy. Second, it is a "collecting" type of activity which seems to be part of my personality make-up as well. Third, it has allowed me to meet a great variety of interesting people, some of whom I do business with and some of whom I have become friends with. Fourth, it is to me a healthy alternative to many of the usual male pursuits such as power boats, hot rods, or guns as a means of recreational and social activity. Fifth, it allows me to share a common interest with my friends, and to get together and play music with them as well as swap guitar stories." Thus Dr. Van Hoose identifies and defines the "recreational/social" aspect of guitar collecting.

Nostalgic Appeal

Most of the collectors surveyed to this point are "Baby Boomers" in their mid- to late thirties, and most of the guitars they are interested in collecting were being manufactured during their adolescent or pre-adolescent years. Tom Van Hoose comments, "Some of us like old guitars because they came from a time in our youth when things were simpler, perhaps more fun, or in some other ways different from the lives that we live today." Timm Kummer, manager of Guitar Trader in New Jersey, is quite knowledgeable about vintage guitars and the vintage guitar market. Timm comments on the nostalgic appeal, "The supply of original instruments is getting lower, and the demand by people who are more and more becoming affluent is getting larger; the only obvious result would be a higher price on old, but selective, guitars. I think the way rock 'n roll memorabilia has skyrocketed at auctions, the respectability of vintage guitars in the same vein is just around the corner. The people who grew up watching Cream and the Allman Brothers are getting out of law school and are able to spend a fair amount on things that in the past have been too costly. I sold a doctor a Fender Stratocaster for $3,000.00 and two years earlier he was in but could not buy the same period Stratocaster (which at the time was $1,750.00) and now he just wanted to have it so he could feel some accomplishment. This may not be a good reason for buying it, and it may not have been the only one, but it certainly was one of them." Brian Brock states, "Possibly a bit of nostalgia is inherent in collecting anything vintage. Trying to live out yesterday in the modern day world." Bob Reed continues, "Apart from guitar, the interest in collecting old things in general seems to be on the increase. There seems to be an increase of late 50's/early 60's automobiles on the roads in Britain these days. Perhaps with more disposable income in people's pockets these days collecting is a luxury more people can afford. I think deep inside every serious collector of any items from the past is a degree of dissatisfaction with things of the present day." About a year ago Bob Reed purchased his pre-CBS Fiesta Red Strat and Bob adds, "It is the guitar that I and thousands of other British guitarists in the early 60's wanted but could never afford at the time." (Hank Marvin of the Shadows played such an instrument.) A. R. Duchossoir has also commented on the nostalgic element in collecting. André states, "In my opinion, 'old guitars' are of interest to a specific generation of people. With time (and money) these people were able to obtain their Holy Grails and you could say they are now living 'happily married' with their cherished babies." It appears this aspect of guitar collecting involves a partial return to adolescence, a desire to locate that dream guitar from the past now that one can afford it. Psychologically this aspect of collecting may provide a defense from or a manifestation of getting older.

Personal Accomplishment

Many of the guitar collectors surveyed have reported some sense of personal accomplishment that has been associated with their collecting and dealing activities. This accomplishment is of the ego identity variety that is truly important to an individual and defines who they are to some degree.

To the question of why guitar collecting is an important part of his life, Steve Melkisethian of Angela Instruments in Maryland responds, "It is my life — I have virtually no other outside interests. Why? I don't know myself. Some ideas — I've always been interested in things, perfection, doing things right (restoration), history, cultural trends, music, and the bizarre. Guitars fit right in!" Steve Melkisethian, "The King of Trash," stocks every conceivable bit and piece from vintage guitars and amps. To read his catalog is truly mind scrambling — "The most extensive inventory in the history of the world."

Timm Kummer responds to the question of why guitar collecting is an important part of his life, "It's one of the few things I know well enough to make a living at and if you can make money with something you love to do then you are doubly blessed. It gives you great satisfaction to educate those who are just starting in the field." Bart Wittrock responds to the same question, "It's something I can excel at, a small piece of history, and the people in general are great and dedicated."

These last few aspects of OGM may be seen as contradictory in that they appear healthy! Could there really be sane reasons for a person to collect old guitars? Collectors have discussed the importance of preserving the instruments for future generations, and they have demonstrated various constructive manifestations of their involvement in old guitars. Few of the collectors are able to identify the unconscious sexual significance of this activity. Could the reasons for desiring old guitars be purely rational? As Sigmund Freud once said to his psychoanalytic colleagues, "Sometimes a guitar is just a guitar" or something to that effect — meaning neurotic conflict and symbolic sexual significance cannot always be attached to an object.

Dr. Van Hoose asserts, "As a hobby, guitar collecting can be a healthy diversion or some form of neurotic gratification. It's my guess that both elements are present, in varying degrees, in all of us who enjoy collecting guitars." Healthy diversion and stimulating prosocial activity versus the dreaded OGM compulsive disorder. Which is the primary motivating force behind personal guitar collections? The dilemma remains unsettled. Could it really be that guitar collecting is essentially a rational and healthy human activity that does not involve vast amounts of unconscious sexual significance and neurotic gratification? — Naw.

 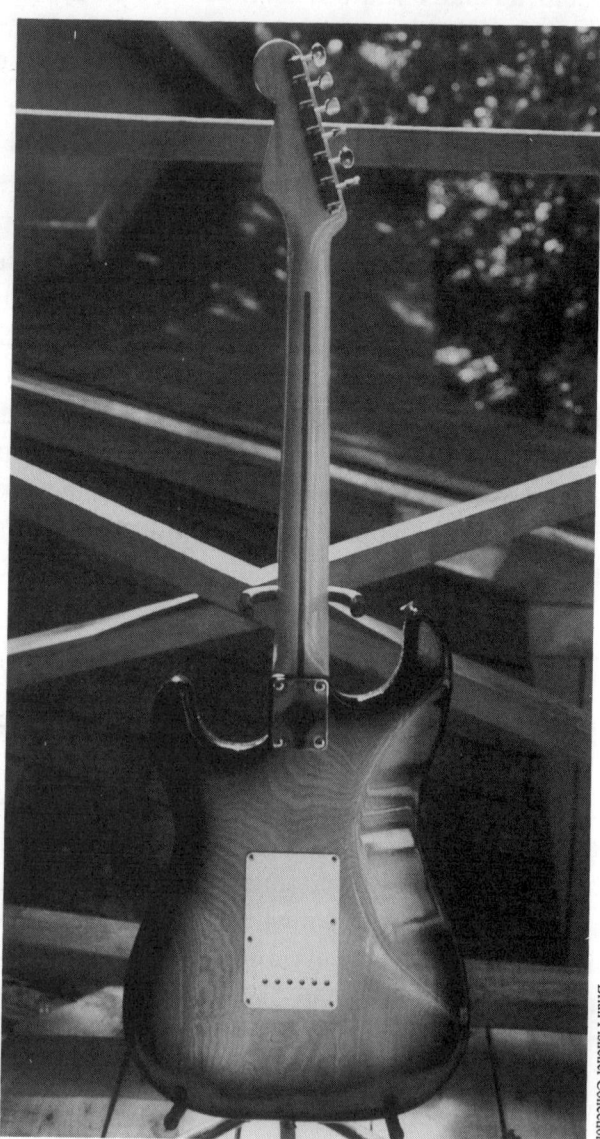

Near Mint 1954 Stratocaster in original Form Fit case.
Note figured ash body.

An original Gibson Flying V- taking off from a stack of Fender Tweed and tolex cases

Gibson 1959 blonde Switchmaster with PAF's

Custom Color Jazzmasters - If only you could see the Fiesta Red, Teal Green, Burgundy Mist with gold parts, etc.

GUITAR TERMINOLOGY

Guitar enthusiasts like other collectors groups have evolved their own jargon over the years. This chapter will cover a basic glossary of guitar slang. It is necessary to acquire a working vocabulary of these terms to be able to function in the guitar collecting world. Some of these terms refer to specific instruments or features of guitars manufactured by a certain maker, while other terms are more general in their usage. When a term's use typically refers to a specific maker, the company's name will precede the term's definition.

ABR-1 — **Gibson**, marking on the underside of early Tune-o-matics.

A-Series — **Gibson**, serial number system which began in 1947 and was discontinued about 1960. These numbers appeared on the labels of hollow-body guitars.

action — The playing "feel" of a guitar. Often refers to the distance between the strings and the frets.

actionflo nut — **Gretsch**, a zero fret introduced on Atkins models in '59 to replace the metal nut; found on all other models subsequent to this.

"Adjustamatic" bridge — **Gretsch**, a bridge design introduced in the 1970's which was similar to Gibson's tune-o-matic.

Alnico — **Gibson**, with respect to Gibson, this magnet composition identifier refers to single coil Gibson pickups with rectangular pole-pieces and black plastic covers.

anodized — **Fender**, gold colored metal pickguard used by Fender in the late 1950's on some guitars.

arch-top — Acoustic guitar with a curved top usually featuring F holes.

arrow control knobs — **Gretsch**, metal control knobs used on electrics until sometime in 1957.

Autumnglo — **Rickenbacker**'s name for a brown sunburst finish.

Bakelite — **Fender**, name used to refer to the earliest plastic-type parts which tend to deteriorate more than later materials (pickup covers and knobs on early Strats, and pickguards on Broadcasters, early Telecasters and Esquires, for example).

bat-wing — Pertains to specific head stock shapes usually referring to certain Epiphones.

belly-bridge — **Martin**, replaced the pyramid type in 1929. Featured a curved "belly" below the string pins.

Bigsby — Shorthand for the vibrola unit designed by Paul Bigsby.

binding — Refers to the edging trim used on the fingerboard or body.

Black Beauty — **Gibson**, nickname for early black finish Les Paul custom.

blond	Natural finish which allows the wood grain to show through.
bound	Refers to a neck or body with binding.
bout	The upper or lower dimension or curved sides of a guitar.
bullet truss rod	**Fender**, refers to a type of truss rod adjustment rod that protrudes through the headstock (first appeared in 1971).
Burst	**Gibson**, nickname for 1958 to 1960 Sunburst Les Paul standard.
CAR	**Fender**, abbreviation for candy apple red custom color.
CBS	**Fender**, refers to Fender guitars made after the sale of Fender to Columbia Broadcasting Systems, Inc. in January, 1965.
CBS logo	**Fender**, headstock decal which was bolder and black with a thin gold outline. Introduced in mid-1968.
Cadillac tailpiece	**Gretsch**, the gold-plated, extension tail on the Falcons and Penguins that bears a Cadillac-looking "V"-shaped chevron and a stylized "G" in its motif.
cat's eye	**Gretsch**, refers to the shape of the sound hole on Gretsch arch top guitars.
center pocket	**Fender**, the first rectangular "tweed" case with the storage pocket in the middle of the case. (Replaced by a case with the pocket in the lower leftcorner in mid-1955).
Charlie Christian pickup	**Gibson**, mid-1930's Gibson pickups used on the 1936 ES-150 and other models; so named because of Christian's use of such.
clay dots	**Fender**, fingerboard position markers of a matte white appearance used from 1959 to early 1965.
cloud-shaped inlays	**Gretsch**, also known as "humped blocks" type of fingerboard inlay.
collector's guitar	An established make and model of a collector's guitar in original, unaltered condition.
Country Gent	**Gretsch**, refers to the Gretsch Chet Atkins Country Gentleman model.
cowboy case	**Gretsch**, the cream-colored tolex hard shell optionally issued with Western-motif guitars in the 1950's.
cows and cactus inlay	**Gretsch**, the engraving found in the fingerboard inlays of Western-appointed guitars depicting cows' heads and cacti.
curley	**Gibson**, refers to a type of maple with a prominent grain pattern. Also called flame or tiger maple.

custom color	**Fender**, special order solid color (as opposed to sunburst or blond) finish.
cut	Short for cutaway.
D-size	**Martin**, stands for "Dreadnought."
dome knob	**Fender**, refers to the domed top type metal control knobs that were used on early Telecasters (later knobs had a flatter top).
dot-marker	**Gibson**, see dot-neck.
dot-neck	**Gibson**, usually a nickname for 1958 to early 1960's ES-335's so named because of the use of simple dot position markers on the fingerboard. Also as a reference to other guitars with dot markers.
double white coils	**Gibson**, refers to the color of humbucking pickup coil bobbins. Originally with respect to PAFs.
ES	**Gibson**, electric Spanish.
electromatic	**Gretsch**, a generic term referring to an electrified group of instruments in the early postwar era.
electrotone hollowbody	**Gretsch**, the semi-hollow body design introduced in late 1961 which has closed, simulated or inlaid, not real, f-holes.
Epi	Short for Epiphone.
F.O.N.	**Gibson**, factory order number, a code stamped on the inside of the guitars which aids in dating.
f-hole	A sound hole that is shaped like an f.
F-Series	**Fender**, refers to a CBS/Fender series of serial numbers that utilizes six digits on the neck plate as well as a larger reverse F stamped on the plate (1965-1976).
"filter-tron"	**Gretsch**, humbucking type of double coil Gretsch pickup that appears in three versions: pre-patent applied for (unlabelled PAF) (1957-1958), patent applied for (1958-60), and patent number (1960-1970).
Fireglo	**Rickenbacker's** name for a red sunburst finish.
fixed arm bigsby	**Gretsch**, a Bigsby vibrato tailpiece on which the tremolo arm cannot be swung out of the player's way; found on Gretsch models until sometime in 1956.
flat-top	An acoustic guitar with a flat face; usually has a round sound hole.
flat-top pickup	**Fender**, early Esquire, Broadcaster, and Telecaster bridge pickup with level polepieces.

floating bridge	**Gretsch**, also known as the "tuning fork" bridge introduced about 1965.
Florentine	Pointed style of guitar cutaway.
form fit	**Fender**, earliest Fender case that was formed in the shape of the guitar.
fretless wonder	**Gibson**, another nickname for early black finish Les Paul Custom; a reference to small squarish shaped frets used by Gibson.
G-brand	**Gretsch**, as in branding iron, a large G burned into the finish. Also used to refer loosely to the Model 6120 from 1955-56.
G-indent control knobs	**Gretsch**, metal control knobs used onGretsch electrics from sometime in 1957 until sometime in 1967 having an impressed arrow and an impressed "G."
G-tailpiece	**Gretsch**, tailpiece with a G shape within. (Also see Cadillac tailpiece).
gold parts	**Fender**, refers to special order gold plated metal parts on Fender guitars.
gold top	**Gibson**, Les Paul model with a metallic gold painted front.
green pickguard	**Fender**, refers to the earliest three-ply celluloid pickguard which had a greenish tint and was discontinued after early 1965.
Gretsch Dynasonic	**Gretsch**'s name for DeArmond pickups which were used from the late 1940's to about 1957.
hardtail	**Fender**, non-tremdo Stratocasters, also see non-trem.
herringbone	**Martin**, sometimes used to refer specifically to pre-War D-28's. In general, refers to the pattern of inlaid marquetry trim used on Martins.
Hilo 'Tron	**Gretsch**, single coil Gretsch pickup first used in the early 1960's.
J-bass	**Fender**, nickname for Jazz bass.
Jag	**Fender**, nickname for Jaguar.
jewelled knobs	**Gretsch**, the rhinestone and pearl encrusted control knobs that grace the White Falcon and White Penguin.
Korina	**Gibson**, trade name for African Limba wood (similar to mahogany) used on Flying V's, Explorers and some lap steels.
LPB	**Fender**, abbreviation for Lake Placid blue custom color.
L-Series	**Fender**, refers to a series of serial numbers that was preceded by an L then five digits (1963-1965).

large headstock	**Fender**, the larger headstocks that were used on CBS (1966) Fender guitars.
Leo-Series	**Fender**, see L-series.
Les Paul TV	**Gibson**, TV refers to a specific "limed mahogany" yellowish color finish.
lipstick pickup	Type of Danelectro single coil pickup encased in a chrome tube.
Lloyd Loar Label	**Gibson's** paper label from the early 1920's featuring the signature of Lloyd Loar.
M-size	**Martin**, grand auditorium.
Mapleglo	**Rickenbacker's** name for a natural finish.
Mary Kay	**Fender**, refers to a blond Stratocaster with gold parts, so designated by Mary Kay's use of such a guitar in early Fender catalogs.
Melita bridge	**Gretsch**, tune-o-matic type of bridge used until the mid-1950's.
Mickey Mouse ears	**Gibson**, refers to the shape of the "horns" on the early 335's, 45's, and 55's which were more rounded than subsequent ones.
neo-classic inlays	**Gretsch**, also known as half moon, thumb nail, or thumb print type of fingerboard position marker inlay.
New York Martins	**Martin**, generally refers to Martins produced before 1898.
Nitron	**Gretsch**, the plastic material used for Gretsch drum coverings, sparkle tops, some duo jets and gold sparkle binding.
non-trem	**Fender**, Stratocasters that are not equipped with the "synchronized tremdo."
OM-size	**Martin**, orchestra model.
orange label	**Gibson**, orange colored oval label used by Gibson from the mid 1950's to the late 1960's or so.
Orville label	**Gibson**, label which featured a picture of Orville Gibson.
P-90	**Gibson**, single coil Gibson pickup with a black or cream colored plastic cover. Can also be found with a chrome cover.
PAF	**Gibson**, refers to Gibson's original (patent applied for) humbucking pickups (1957 to about 1962). Identified by decal on bottom.

P-Bass	**Fender**, nickname for Precision Bass.
paper	Refers to guitar catalogs, tags, brochures, manuals and other "paper" collectibles.
patent number	**Gibson**, refers to Gibson's humbucking pickups after the early sixties when it received the patent number decal.
pearl	Refers to mother of pearl or abalone inlay.
pinetop	**Gretsch**, any Gretsch solidbody using pine as the top wood, usually a Model 6130 RoundUp.
player's guitar	An established make and model of a collectors guitar that has been abused or modified in some way to significantly reduce its collectors value, but not its utility value.
pot	Short for potentiometer (volume and tone controls).
pre-CBS	**Fender**, guitars made before the sale to CBS.
pre-war	Refers to instruments (usually acoustic) that were produced before the beginning of World War II.
project-o-sonic	**Gretsch**'s stereo guitar designation.
purfling	The inlaid decorative trim around the edges of the guitar's sides and sound hole.
pyramid bridge	**Martin**, earlier rectangular bridges that have pyramid shapes on the ends.
recessed edge control knobs	**Gretsch**, aluminum control knobs with a chamfered edge and a stencilled "G" on top.
Res-o-glass	**National Guitar's** name for their fiberglass guitar bodies.
reverse Firebird	**Gibson**, the original style Gibson Firebird in which the horn of the cutaway on the treble side is larger (reverse of the more common practice).
Rick	Short for **Rickenbacker.**
sb	Abbreviation for Sunburst.
SG	**Gibson**, solid guitar, refers to the type of Gibson double cutaway solid body with sharp horns of the cutaway.
SG Les Paul	**Gibson**, the earliest SG shaped Les Paul customs, standards and Jr's. (early sixties SG's that still carried the Les Paul designation).
scalloped bracing	**Martin**, also referred to as "voiced" bracing. Lighter x-bracing used before late 1944.

side-to-side vibrola	**Gibson**, early 60's vibrato that functioned in a side to side fashion.
signature-signpost pickguard	**Gretsch**, the pickguard used on the Chet Atkins series bearing the "Chet Atkins" signature inside a ranch's signpost.
skunk-stripe	**Fender**, the darker (usually walnut) strip of wood that is used to fill the truss rod channel in the neck.
slab-board	**Fender**, rosewood fingerboard which was thicker than later ones and milled flat on the neck — used originally from 1959 to mid-1962.
small headstock	**Fender**, the earliest headstocks used on Fender Stratocasters and Jazzmasters (1954-1965).
snakehead	A nickname for a type of headstock that is narrower at the top.
snowflake inlay	**Martin**, refers to fingerboard inlays that appear like snowflakes.
soap bar	**Gibson**, another name for P-90 pickups.
solidbody	A guitar with a body constructed of solid wood.
space-control bridge	**Gretsch**, also known as roller bridge. Used from the mid-1950's to about 1958.
spaghetti logo	**Fender**, refers to the earliest Fender headstock decal logo which featured a slim script style used until mid-1964.
stack-knob	**Fender**, earliest production model Jazz Bass with tandem mounted tone and volume controls.
staggered pole pieces	**Fender**, refers to pickups with pole pieces of differing heights.
stop tailpiece	**Gibson's** dual function bridge/tailpiece unit.
Strat	**Fender**, nickname for Stratocaster.
sunburst	A guitar finish that is shaded from a darker color on the edges to a lighter color in the center, usually using two or three colors.
"Super 'Tron"	**Gretsch**, pickup introduced in the early 1960's which used "blades" instead of adjustable screws.
synchromatic	**Gretsch**, a generic term referring to instruments and appointments found before the modern era of the early-mid '50s.

synchrosonic	**Gretsch**, the stair-step-style bridge and tailpiece found on pre-war and early post-war synchromatic archtops.
T-roof logo	**Gretsch**, logo which was introduced after 1953 and used on most guitars.
"T-zone"	**Gretsch**, a feature from about 1965 which was intended to improve the intonation by slightly slanted frets after the 15th position.
tags	Refers to the original printed materials that were supplied with an instrument, usually a small manual and cards that hung from the tuners.
Tele	**Fender**, nickname for Telecaster.
telescoping arm vibrato	**Gretsch**, the Burns-made vibrato found on post-1964 guitars with a trem arm that pulls out of housing in the arm itself.
tenor	A four string guitar with a banjo style neck.
three bolt neck	**Fender**, refers to the three (as compared to four) bolt neck fastening system Fender introduced in 1971.
tilt-neck	**Fender**, neck angle adjustment system introduced in 1971.
top-hat switch	**Fender**, type of plastic switch handle used on Telecasters and Esquires which resembles a top hat.
transition logo	**Fender**, used from mid-1964 to mid-1968. Fender's script style which was larger than the spaghetti style, but still featured gold or silver lettering with a black outline.
trapeze	Refers to a type of tailpiece that is hinged at he body.
tune-o-matic	**Gibson**, name for a bridge which featured intonation adjustments for each string.
tweed	**Fender**, airplane luggage linen covering used for Fender guitar cases and amp coverings during the 1950's. "Tweed" is often used to refer specifically to tweed covered amps.
unsculpted rings	**Gretsch**, the pickup surrounds made from flat plastic found on late 1957 and early 1958 guitars.
v-neck	Also known as "boat neck." Refers to the shape or contour of the neck.
Venetian	Rounded style of guitar cutaway.
vertical logo	**Gretsch**, the gold sparkle "Gretsch" logo used on Falcons and Penguins which was oriented up and down on the guitars' pegheads.
Wildwood	**Fender**, refers to a beechwood injected with dye finished guitar (late 1960's).
zebra	**Gibson**, refers to the color (1 black and 1 white) of humbucking pickup coil bobbins, originally with respect to PAF's.

1959 Fender Telecaster-Strings terminate at the bridge on this example and don't follow through to back of body.

1958 & 1959 Gibson Les Paul Customs "Black Beauty's"

1959 Gibson Les Paul Standard. Note: Even Tiger-striped maple.

Early 1960's Les Paul Custom when the "SG" was still called a Les Paul model.

All guitars this page courtesy of Vic Da Pra Collection

THE THRILL OF VINTAGE AND THE AGONY OF DEFRET

(Guitar Collector Survey, Report 3,)

At a recent guitar show, a well-known and likable collector was observed to be uncharacteristically skeptical and even antagonistic to a dealer. As the eager merchant proudly displayed and offered to the individual a "dead mint" vintage guitar, the collector was overheard to respond: "If I hear the words 'dead mint' one more time - I think I'll puke! - the only thing 'killer' about that guitar is the price tag!"

A dramatic increase in the annoying and downright disturbing aspects of Old Guitar Mania (OGM) have been documented by the Guitar Collector Survey. Consider the common parlance of the collecting business: Pre-CBS, PAF, Custom Color, dot-neck, stack-knob, slab-board, gold-top, Burst, dead mint, etc. If any of these terms that once stimulated an emotional thrill is beginning to result in a negative association, mild annoyance or, more intensely (like the anonymous collector), a sick feeling in your stomach - you are also experiencing the negative side effects of OGM.

The Guitar Collector Survey was initiated a number of years ago to examine the question, "Why do we go nuts for vintage guitars?" The question was evaluated from the standpoint of traditional psychological theories and "collector generated categories" culled from the responses of leading collectors across the country (and Europe). The first category is the "dream guitar" notion that stems from musical interests and the search for the proper instrument. This search can apparently lead to an "addiction/ compulsion" aspect of pursuing guitars. Within the activity of collecting are various psychologically meaningful aspects which have been identified as: "recreational/social," "nostalgic appeal," and "personal accomplishment." These categories have been explored and generally define the positive psychological and emotional attraction to vintage guitars. But, as is true with any love object, the flip side of frustration, anger and aversion cannot be denied, and deserves further investigation with respect to vintage guitars. Our efforts to acquire the objects of our affection are often frustrated by roadblocks or, once possessed, the object does not satisfy our expectations.

Burstserk and Stratsophrenic, not to mention Telepathic, collectors continue to be in evidence, but the intensity of their OGM symptoms may be lessening due to rational thinking possibly brought about by the down side of the collectors' mania. Thus, in this installment of the Guitar Collectors Survey, we will report on the responses from an ever increasing data pool of collectors to the question, "What do you find to be the most annoying aspect of collecting and the vintage guitar field in general?"

The responses of the collectors have been categorized under three broad areas of annoyance:

Unethical Selling

John Sprung, owner of the American Guitar Center in Maryland and professional musician since 1969, responds to the question on the most annoying aspect of collecting. John writes, "Being taken advantage of when the seller knows I can't go on living without buying. I also don't like a lot of the questionable deals offered to me." John nicely conveys the emotional intensity involved in acquiring a piece and how the collector's "need" can be exploited by the seller. Jeff Gray, a criminal defense attorney from California and Fender collector, is also concerned about the ethical issues. Jeff's response to the annoyance question is: "Pieced together instruments, people who misrepresent originality." Jeff writes, "The vintage guitar is a masterpiece instrument that produces the greatest tone. Quality is what it is all about." Within his concept of the vintage guitar, originality is critical.

Gil Southworth with an original clear lefty SG
(1962-63, no visible serial number)

Another respondent writing from the dealer's perspective is the colorful Gil Southworth of Southworth Guitars in Washington, D.C. Gil has been known to "punish the brown party truck drivers" by buying so many guitars. Gil states, "The one thing that really annoys me, and I would like to preface it by saying it's not the prices — that never phases me in the least. I never hang up the phone and say, 'What a suburban melodrama; this guy wants a Frey boot box full of gold bullion.' What really saddens me is when a person calls and offers me a guitar, we negotiate the price, and the guy doesn't send it to me! People want a free estimate, but will go through the motions of selling an instrument and never follow through on it." Gil's observation illustrates that the seller's ethical conduct is a central issue to both dealers and collectors. As the sequestered but ever present collector, Alan Hardke, writes, "Now that condition and pedigree are established as major concerns for instrument collectors, I see dealer [seller] integrity as the next hurdle if this hobby is to expand." Alan further acknowledges from a position of extensive experience that many responsible guitar collectors and dealers indeed exist and are very much appreciated. Hardke and the other survey participants are interested in the continued development of the guitar collecting enterprise. An accepted theory of development states that with increased development comes increased differentiation. The difference between a slightly altered instrument and a completely original one is great to the collector, and not a matter to be neglected, or worse, misrepresented. Of course the ethical choice is fraught with temptation as the profit differential between the slightly altered and completely original is also great and will likely be increasing.

C. William Kaman II - Presently interested in building "New" dream guitars. President of Kaman Music Corp. Guitar & Car collector.

Know-it-all Personalities

Many survey participants made similar comments regarding this annoying but apparently common phenomenon. C. William Kaman II, president of Kaman Music Corporation, defines this category by his comment: "The most annoying aspect of collecting is having to deal with the self-appointed know-it-alls who really don't know much at all." Two private collectors answered this question in very similar ways. Joe Stefanini, an auto parts manager from Aliquippa, Pennsylvania, writes, "Dealers or people who misrepresent what they're selling or don't know what they're talking about." Brian Fischer, president of Ear Craft in Dover, New Hampshire, is most annoyed

Brian Fischer with 1964 Firebird. One of many guitars in his amazing collection.

about "Dealing with unethical people and people who do not know what they are talking about, but insist they do!" Another nearly identical response comes from guitar repairman and builder Ron Lira of Honest Ron's Guitars in Oklahoma. Ron writes, "Most annoying is people with no knowledge of old guitars attempting to bullshit you! Terrible!" A final collector comment in this category comes from Skip Henderson of City Lights Music in New Jersey. Skip says the most enjoyable aspect of collecting is "finding blue telecasters" and the most annoying is encountering "non-players with more money than brains — posers."

What is going on here with such widespread and consistent perceptions? A simple interpretation would be that a good number of individuals with questionable sales ethics and limited knowledge are attempting to cash in on a growing market. This is undoubtedly true in some instances, but is not the only possibility. Collectors, dealers and players have a great deal of ego-involvement with their guitar related activities. A person's very identity and self-esteem can become associated with knowledge and expertise, based unfortunately on too little experience, and if confronted the individual may rigorously defend his or her information in a face saving gesture. The amount of knowledge and first hand experience needed to acquire genuine authority status is vast and most true experts (more secure in their position) will reject a "know-it-all" posture.

High Prices

What more can be said about the high prices of vintage guitars? Plenty! Tim Matyas, a collector and guitar/amplifier repairman at Guitar Gallery in Pennsylvania, writes, "The most annoying aspect of collecting to me is how expensive these things really are. I have to balance out all the different uses for the money when I'm looking for a piece. It bothers me sometimes to think how much my collection is worth (especially when bills are due, etc.). The reality of a cheaper, new guitar is always there." Tim's wife, Robin (not your typical guitar widow, being a professional player herself), adds, "As far as Tim's collecting old guitars, I'm just glad it's guitars and not some-

Tim Matyas with one of Vic's bursts. (He does have one of his own, but this isn't it.)

thing else. He could be an alcoholic or a drug user or worse. Although, maybe being an alcoholic or a drug user would be cheaper!"

Marc Newman, one of the publishers of the Guitar Digest, and college business and accounting instructor, is also concerned about escalating prices. To the survey question, Marc answers, "The *prices* of

Marc Newman, co-publisher of Guitar Digest and co-sponsor of Ohio Guitar Shows.

so-called vintage guitars. In this market, like many others, there are collectors with the financial resources to drive the price structure all to hell — when 50's Strats are commanding 4 and 5 thousand, the market's all screwed up. I don't mean to imply that 50's Strats aren't wonderful (because they are!), but I'm just not sure they're worth $5000." The next respondent, Richard R. Smith, is a player, author and widely respected authority on vintage guitars and amps (the R. stands for Rare?). Richard writes, "Many people have come to believe that old is always better. Some old guitars are worth collecting, some are worth playing, and some are worth forgetting. I like Silvertone guitars; I paid $10 for mine at a garage sale. And certainly some Gibson models are highly desirable; I paid a lot for my 1960 sunburst. But I was in a store recently that had a Silvertone and a non-reverse Firebird *locked up* in a glass case. I won't tell you what the guy thought the instruments were worth, but the prices were ridiculous. At ridiculous prices, all old guitars are worth forgetting." Paul Day is a survey participant from England who specializes in collecting the "forgettable" guitars! Paul says, "So often prices are inflated to a ridiculously inflated degree because of misinformation, or simply because the instruments are 'old' and therefore 'rare' and therefore 'sought-after.' This especially hurts when one is collecting 'fun' guitars at 'fun' prices! Paul continues, "Most of my collection could be termed failures, I suppose, the 'also ran's,' the ones who just didn't make it into the big league. So many of them are great guitars in my opinion, and some did sell well, but most weren't everyone's (or anyone's in some cases!) idea of the perfect electric." Which guitars are collectible would appear to be determined by the individual. One man's Teisco is another man's Tele.

This investigation of the most annoying aspects of collecting serves to illustrate the complexity of the field and diversity of participants. The Guitar Collector Survey has queried a wide range of collectors over the years, with varied interests, level of resources, and commitment to the collecting enterprise. Neither the collectors' lives nor the field of guitar collecting remains static; both will continue to evolve. The end point of an individual's development with respect to guitar collecting will vary from person

Paul Day - Holding aloft a lovely old Tokai Humming bird, c 1968

to person. A number of guitar collectors who were at one time very serious about the hobby have lost this passion and sold their collections. A significant example of such is past survey participant Vic Da Pra. Vic recently sold off his extensive collection and is no longer looking for one that's cleaner and curlier than the last! C. William Kaman II writes, "My tastes have changed. I basically play the same 10 guitars and the others take up space. In the last 2 years I've been selling off the collection and putting the money to better use; Vintage Cadillacs." Kaman continues, "My final comment on my guitar collecting is part of what I said before and part from a BB King song, 'Once you have two of everything you've ever wanted...the thrill is gone.'"

The thrill may be gone for some, but others such as James Werner (the Iowa recluse with a hay wagon load of Fenders and keeper of THE LIST), will likely never lose their devotion to collecting. The hobby of guitar collecting will survive and, hopefully, experience continued developmental progress. Alan Hardke offers a couple of thoughtful suggestions. He writes, "Collectors should be informed and only buy what is worth collecting, leaving the altered pieces at low prices for the players. Make up your mind, are you a 'player,' 'collector' or 'dealer,' i.e. 'I'm a player just looking for a good Strat, but it must be Fiesta Red with gold hardware having never seen a soldering iron since Fullerton' get real!!" The categorization of an individual as a player, collector or dealer is not a simple matter, as a person could progress through stages or wear two hats. But the classification of guitars that are collectible (condition and pedigree) could be somewhat easier, and a subject deserving continued effort. The differentiation of guitars as collectible or not is subject to fads and fluctuations and, of course, relates to the price structure situation. The law of supply and demand will ultimately be determinate in the price formulation.

So, we don't go as nuts for vintage guitars as we once did! There are a number of individuals that even appear to be cured of their Old Guitar Mania! But, there is a maturing and developing guitar collecting enterprise in evidence. Increased differentiation between guitars as collectible or not, increased knowledge on the part of buyers and sellers, and a push for a higher level of ethical conduct is underway. All of these elements will enrich and advance the field. Some collectors will drop out, newcomers will contract the mania, but the hardcore will persevere and smile in agreement with Alan Hardke's conclusion, "Still the most fun you can have with your clothes on is playing the right guitar through the right amp and sharing some new discovery with other enthusiasts."

"What more does a man need?"
Skip Henderson's 1961 Bigsby

Gold! The earliest Les Paul Standard ('52) and Gibson ES295, featured the same gold finish and the Les Paul designed trapeze bar combination bridge/tailpiece.

Highly Figured Flame maple 1959 Les Paul Standard

1958 Les Paul Sunburst. Highly figured grain is the name of the game in the burst competition.

Reverse Gibson Firebird V in custom color. Reverse Firebirds were introduced in mid 1963 and discontinued in 1965.

Gibson "Dot Neck" ES-335. Blonde. 1958 birdseye maple top. Dot markers, PAF humbucking pickups and Stop tailpiece define the breed.

Mint. 1958 Les Paul gold top with PAF's and dark colored back.

MAINTAINING YOUR COLLECTION

Basics

One of the greatest obstacles to building a guitar collection is resisting the considerable urge to sell. How many times have you heard a fellow player say, "If I only would have kept that guitar?" While keeping all the guitars a person has ever owned is at least impractical, an essential task of collecting is to hold on to the choicest pieces. This most basic aspect of maintenance, or preservation, is not as easily mastered as it would seem for various reasons. Much of the thrill in the collecting business is in the hunt and not the hoarding. Of course, considerable satisfaction can result from the joy of possession. But, many of the prime collectors guitars are not necessarily the best "player's guitars." If for no other reason than cosmetic condition and the risk of damage, many of the best examples are infrequently played. Therefore, it's easier to sell a guitar that is seldom played, especially one that has increased dramatically in value. The successful collector will need to have patience and work towards a long term goal. Many of the collectors that have participated in the collector survey have specialized in certain instruments or established a specific theme (custom color Fenders, Gibson Super 400's, etc.). The defining of definite parameters to an individual's collection will help to focus and direct future acquisitions and a goal of collecting the finest examples of a series will require time. The rewards (both financial and psychological) for patience and perseverance will be considerable.

Storage and Security

For the most part, guitars do not require very specialized storage. It is important to avoid extremes of heat or cold and stick to room temperature conditions. Corresponding extremes in humidity can also be a problem, especially dryness with respect to acoustics. In hot, dry climates an in-case humidifier may be needed. Wet, humid basements should also be avoided for obvious reasons. Many collectors simply place their guitars in a closet, under a bed, in a cabinet or specialized area of the house. The guitars should be securely in their cases and preferably upright. Collectors differ on the de-tuning issue. Some do not de-tune the guitars at all, others recommend de-tuning for longer term storage.

While a number of individuals with extensive collections have their guitars stored at some location other than their residence with differing levels of security, many collectors have no choice other than their residence. In this case it is wise to be prudent in several respects. Be creative in the placement of the instruments. For example, it may be wise not to have them all in one spot. To put them in unusual locations when away for a period of time is another idea. It is safer not to sell guitars from your residence, or to display a collection for strangers or casual acquaintances. This thinking may sound a bit paranoid to some, but the reality is that guitars are easy targets for theft. They are very portable and not difficult to sell.

Collectors will need to obtain insurance for their collections. It is unlikely that an individual's standard homeowners or renters insurance package will cover a collector's guitar to any significant extent. The collector will need to add special coverage for the guitars as an addendum to his or her existing policy. This guide recommends that the collector contact his or her insurance agent, as each person's situation is different and requires individualized advice. In virtually all cases, though, an itemized appraisal will be required. This inventory will need to include a brief, but specific, description of each item and be certified by an established dealer or knowledgeable individual agreeable to all parties. Many guitar dealers provide this service for a certain charge per instrument. The collector would only need to provide them with a clear picture of the guitar. This could be a rather expensive way to go for a large collection, though, as the values will need to be updated on a yearly basis or so. There are other alternatives such as having a collector friend do the appraisal. Don't be hesitant to ask around to establish a mutually acceptable arrangement.

The collector should retain a copy of the appraisal (including description and value) in a safe place, presumably not at the residence. Corresponding pictorial or video documentation will also be helpful if it includes a degree of detail which could be used to identify stolen property. The very idea of attempting to document ownership in the unthinkable experience of the loss of collectible instrument is a sickening thought. To the collector the guitar would, of course, be immediately recognizable, if it were to be found. But, the authorities involved will need some proof, which should be able to be documented by the basics of make, model, serial number, etc. Established theft prevention techniques, such as marking the item with a person's social security number, are clearly out of the question in the case of collector's guitars. Some collectors have written their name and other pertinent information on a slip of paper or masking tape and attached it in a control cavity or within the hollow body of a guitar. Such a simple and harmless practice could pay off.

It will take time and effort to provide reasonable protection for your collection, but it's really a small investment to make considering the larger investment at stake.

Restoration

The subject of restoration in the vintage guitar field is a delicate one. As this guide has previously stated, the most desirable instruments are in completely original condition. In fact, the very definition of a "collectors guitar" refers to an unaltered instrument with its original parts and finish in pristine condition. With such an instrument there is no need for restoration and any inclination towards modification should be strongly resisted. Even changing parts and pickups that could later be reversed should be avoided as the unoriginal solder joint can devalue the instrument and would matter considerably to some collectors. The larger issue involved is the defacing of a vintage instrument. The guitar's existence will outlast the owner's in most cases. The present day "caretaker" of the article has a very real obligation to respect and conserve the instrument's integrity, beauty and originality for future generations. Such acts of preservation in the service of history, music and art are the most worthy aspects of collecting.

In the real world of collecting, though, the completely original instrument is not as commonly encountered as ones that have already been modified or are in need of repair. In most cases it will be desirable to return the instrument to as near original condition as possible. Unoriginal parts can be replaced with original ones. These parts are becoming increasingly difficult to find, but given time and money, most items should be possible to locate. Many guitars will have had their finish stripped or exhibit a poor refinish. These instruments can be professionally refinished to an original factory specification color. Such restorations will generally increase the value of the instrument somewhat, and its attractiveness substantially.

A good cleaning and polishing can sometimes dramatically improve the appearance of a neglected instrument. Even with such a simple task, a good deal of care should be taken not to damage the finish or parts. Rusted or corroded metal parts can be polished somewhat, but their appearance can usually not be improved substantially without replating, which is definitely not recommended.

Other problems are more difficult to correct. A guitar may need a fret job, a neck set, or have a dead pickup. The pickup may be able to be repaired, but in most cases will have an open coil and require a rewind. These major repairs, like a vintage refinish, will demand the skill of an expert.

The decision to repair or restore and in what fashion will generally be determined on an individual basis. Most decisions will require some thought and possible consultation. Any of the guitar collector survey participants mentioned in this guide would be a good source of information regarding resources and referrals for qualified vintage guitar repair and restoration specialists.

The decision whether to repair or restore at all is difficult in some cases. Most guitars, no matter how worn and battered, will still be worth more left as they are as long as they are still functional. If the instrument is not playable in its present condition, the decision to alter it in the service of functionality will usually not be a difficult one to make. In the case of a "player's guitar" that is highly modified (refinished, refretted, modified pickups, etc.) the decision to change it is not critical. But, to refinish one of Jimi's burnt Strats — never!, or what if a pickup went dead on Bloomfield's sunburst? The answers are not always easy.

Miscellany

To be able to maintain your guitar collecting activities you must first maintain your interest and enthusiasm for the subject. Guitar collecting is an intellectual and emotional venture. More than a few individuals have experienced "burnout" after earlier phases of stimulation and acute episodes of "Old Guitar Mania." The serious collector will need to learn ways to increase frustration tolerance, be patient and maintain an optimistic attitude in the face of high prices, unethical sellers and the like. The collector will benefit from not losing sight of his or her initial love of the instruments, the music and the meaningful personal relationships developed with fellow collectors.

Other avenues to sustaining and furthering your collecting interests involve the broadening of your acquisitions into the complementary fields of guitar catalogs, amps, and related paraphernalia (tags, cards, picks, promotional materials, etc.) These fields are developing rapidly and worthy of book length treatments themselves. In general, the same collecting rules apply such as pedigree, condition, and originality.

Guitar amp collecting has been increasing in popularity in recent years. Fender amps have always been in vogue from the early "Tweed" airplane luggage linen covered examples to the later black face models of the 1960's. Other amplifiers are desirable for various reasons. Some collectors strive to acquire guitar and amp combinations as originally offered by the manufacturer, such as the pairing of the Gretsch Round Up guitar and matching Gretsch amp in western motif. Other amps are desirable for their distinctive sound such as Marshalls or Magnatone Vibrato models. Sometimes an amp gains acceptance since it was the first, and perhaps superior in some ways, like the brown Tolex covered Fender Vibroverbs. In all cases the sounds and historic references are important. Some collectors would argue that the true vintage sound can only be achieved by the combination of the guitar <u>and</u> amp. The guitar amps can provide a larger set of problems than the guitars with respect to maintenance and storage, though.

Paper collecting, as it is called, is also becoming very popular. The reasons an individual has to seek these materials are varied. While not always completely reliable, the amount of information presented in the catalogs, (price lists, color charts, etc.) is extensive and extremely valuable to the guitar historian or enthusiast. Many collectors would like to possess the catalog which depicts their prized guitar and have the tags, warranty cards, and owners manual that were originally provided by the manufacturer. Some truly coveted collector's guitars are found with the original tags, manual, polishing cloth and strap in the case, completely undisturbed. Such collector's guitars are also essentially unplayed which does not diminish their value. To have any further accompanying articles such as a bill of sale would only serve to heighten the time travelling experience of returning to the year the guitar was new. Some guitar catalogs like the full color, full line Fender offerings have achieved a level of respect in excess of simple accompanying literature. Such promotional materials, as collectible items, may represent the ultimate in terms of convenience as well as aesthetics.

An extreemly rare custom color, custom Pre-CBS Telecaster with original strap, polishing cloth and white tolex case.

AFTERWORDS

(Guitar Collector Survey, "Update" Report 4,)

The "Guitar Collector Survey" which was initiated in 1984 by the author in an effort to query a few knowledgeable individuals has developed into a longitudinal look at many of the leading collectors and authorities from around the world. In mid-1990 all of the participants from previous "reports" were asked to submit their comments to the "Guitar Collector Questionnaire, Update" (Appendix C). Six years had passed since the first collectors submitted their comments and the survey was interested in exploring changes that may have transpired in the attitudes and activities of the collectors. In addition, the comments of a couple of prominent individuals in the collecting field were added that were not a part of the original survey. Rather than categorize or analyze the collectors' thoughts, it seemed most instructive and entertaining to run them in their entirety.

The collectors who responded to the update appear in alphabetical order. Their answers to the two update questions:

(1) How have your collecting activities changed since your participation in the survey? Where are you now?, Still collecting?, Current interests, etc.

(2) What are your thoughts or predictions as to the future of the vintage guitar market and the activity of guitar collecting?,

and additional comments are as follows:

Klaus Blasquiz, Musician, Journalist and TV Producer, Paris, France.

(1) "I just finished my book, the one I have been writing for too much time: The Fender Bass Book. It will be published by Hal Leonard in English, and is the result of a long task and a lot of hard [work]. I am still collecting guitars, basses, amps, synthesizers, percussions, and accessories, mostly items bearing names such as: Fender, Gibson, Gretsch, Rickenbacker, Marshall, Vox, Ampeg, etc..."

"The French Ministry of Culture gave me the opportunity to continue further on my strange activities by giving me a 'mission letter.' This is a great chance; they offer me to study a project I am dreaming of for years: a sort of complex dealing with music and electricity surrounding a kind of 'live' museum. There will be a musician's house, a 'musitheque,' an information center (with all facilities such as computers and reprinted documents...), a club for live music, seminars, clinics, master classes and demos, and of course a shop for teaching electronic and 'lutherie' (and to repair or rebuild instruments). As you can see I am pretty much busy..."

(2) "The vintage guitar market will grow in the future, but differently than in the past. One should look at the vintage car market or antique cars and planes to understand that it will be more serious, and more professional than ever. Recently, Sothebys in London have seen a beautiful Strat that used to belong to Jimi Hendrix; it was sold for a fortune, but with respect. And do you remember

George Bush trying to play along with B. B. King? Such events dealing with officials, politicians and THE 'real' big money. Not few dollars for a plank of wood, but consistent sums of money closer to those of the art market. Now we can say that not only these instruments are good for music, witnesses of history, emotional treasures, but also items to make a living (and more) with."

"Once again excuse my English, I do my best to express my feelings and my growing knowledge, but it should be done in French... Since I am not a dealer I'd like you to mention that point: I am a collector, a music lover, a musician, and I am concerned by the money involved with this 'business' only because I have to spend it!"

*   *   *

Vic Da Pra, Musician, Guitar Gallery, Pennsylvania.

(1) "Since starting on collecting again, I now only collect Gibson guitars which were always my first love."

(2) "Guitar collecting has gotten to be a big dollar business. The vintage guitar in today's market is getting to be more of a collectible item than an instrument for use. I, myself, am guilty of this. When I started collecting, it was strictly for use of the instrument, but now the dollar amounts of guitars have gotten so high, I look at them in a more collectible investment kind of way."

*   *   *

Paul Day, Musician, Author, Guitar Historian, Sound Investments, Devon, England.

(1) "Still collecting weirdos, 'character' electrics, etc., but less inclined to buy cheapos that require a lot of work. Now I go for nicer (usually more expensive) examples. Collection total now reduced from 500 down to a more enjoyable and accessible 400 maximum. My tastes are now more 'refined,' but the vintage classics still bore me rigid, I still love those different and alternative makes and models, but now it's the more playable ones!"

(2) "Can't see much change ahead; certain brands and models will come into fashion, then drop, as usual, with prices to match the trends. With the best examples long since bought up, then the player/collector will be able to buy the 'second division' examples, as soon as dealers realize the big money is no longer out there! Hopefully prices will at least level out!"

*   *   *

André Duchossoir, Private Collector, Author, Vintage Guitar Historian/Authority, Paris, France.

(1) "Yes, the bug caught up with me again in late '89. But not on a very large scale like, say before '84. Always Fender electrics, with a renewed interest in collecting 'paper' (i.e. catalogs and brochures.) Actually, this is my main area of investment."

(2) "Apparently it is still going strong, although it's getting more and more pricey. Besides, younger people don't seem to be as keen on it as people in their 30's and 40's. Finally, I wonder whether the feverish activity of Japanese collectors is not the prime factor behind it all in the late 80's!"

*   *   *

George Gruhn, Author, Vintage Guitar Historian/Authority, Gruhn Guitars, Inc., Tennessee.

(1) "Since 1986 the vintage market has changed radically, prices have escalated. Many instruments have doubled in less than a year. While prices were relatively stable from 1976 through 1986, the period from '86 through '90 has been a roller coaster ride. Stratocaster prices went up dramatically and then plunged 40%. Most other prices have gone up and currently remain up. Foreign buyers have a powerful influence in controlling market trends and prices. The number of dealers and number of guitar shows have greatly increased. As the market becomes more lucrative, competition increases. Auction houses such as Sotheby's and Christie's have become active in handling rock and roll memorabilia and some personality associated guitars have brought record auction prices. As a dealer this new climate has increased my business. I am presently in the process of purchasing the building next door to my shop so I can more than double our size."

(2) "I am always hesitant to act as an oracle in predicting the future. I can't say what a loaf of bread will cost in 5 years, let alone what guitars will do in the coming 5 to 10 years. It certainly appears that there is a craze for memorabilia of any kind. Vintage guitars are now priced much higher than a few years ago, but are still relatively inexpensive compared to other collectibles, such as art, vintage automobiles, or historic documents. As long as interest in music remains strong and the world economy is healthy, the guitar market should thrive. The gulf between 'used' and 'vintage collectible' guitars can be expected to grow. For now the market looks crazy but viable."

*   *   *

Norm Harris, Norm's Rare Guitars, California.

(1) "I'm still collecting as avidly as ever. I thought it might wear off by now, but it definitely has not."

(2) "I think the further we get from the date of manufacture, the rarer these instruments become. I think there will always be a demand for good, original examples of classic vintage guitars."

*   *   *

Skip Henderson, City Lights Music, New Jersey.

(1) "I now own 5 guitars: 1961 Bigsby, 1912 Gibson style O, 1968 Tele Thinline — Turquoise (original), 1959 Denelectro, 1964 Duo-Sonic — That's it! Do I need more???"

(2) "Collecting on a number of levels will continue. — Higher level guitar collecting for 90% of the market is doomed as the world economy has taken over."

*   *   *

* * *

Brian Fischer, Ear Craft. New Hampshire.

(1) "Still collecting as much as ever — a true Guitar Pig — hopefully to open a vintage guitar and lit. museum someday. I currently have approximately 500 guitars and 200 amps."

(2) "This is very hard for anyone to predict, but I know the interest is still growing and more people are trying to get involved — it is getting extremely hard to find quality instruments and deal with the large numbers of unknowledgeable people that get misinformation from many sources. It is too bad the market has turned, but it only makes me search harder and try to keep a good attitude. Although the price of guitars is at an all time high, I am still bothered much more by the ethics of the people in the business. It is certainly nothing like it was 5-10 years ago. I could tell many stories in this area of dealing, but it seems the term 'anything goes' sums it up. I'm in hopes better times are on the way and instruments will continue to be found. 'Protect American Heritage — Keep them in the U.S.'"

* * *

"Uncle Lou" Gatanas, Private Collector, New York.

Select quotes from Uncle Lou's responses to the original collector's survey that pertain to his interests and attitudes about collecting:

"My first good guitar was a '71 Strat. I used to play it out front of my house. A neighbor came by and started talking to me one day about his guitars, what kind, how old, how rare, etc. Then I thought, 'Excellent' another universal language. Since then we've gone on any 'guitar safaris.'"

"I don't carry credit cards, but I do carry a shot of my Burst. It has humbled many loud mouthed Charvel Kramer heads! It's also lots of fun watching your investment double and triple."

"Uncle Lou" Gatanas
"Who says you can't take it with you?"

"Given my financial situation, I have to limit my collection to quality not quantity. I only go for killer clean, painfully rare, very desirable pieces. The ultimate would be owning a Korina trio, Explorer, 'V' and Moderne — Keep dreaming!"

"Guitar mania was started by the 'Guitar Gods' Clapton, Page, Hendrix, etc. These guys decided they liked certain guitars and their followers said 'count me in too.' Then supply and demand came into play. As long as people want to emulate their heroes, using the same gear, vintage guitars will always be big."

(2) "Every time I thought the market peaked, it would still go up much higher — so I won't comment!"

* * *

C. William Kaman II, Private Collector, President of Kaman Music Corp., Connecticut.

(1) "After 15 years of collecting and trading, I began to lose interest. I still have about 50 instruments. Kaman Music also bought Hamer guitars in 1988 and since then I've focused more on building 'new' dream guitars that combine the best of the old and new. Other current interests are vintage automobiles."

(2) "As of today in 1990, the market still seems fairly active. It is somewhat of a shame that most of the demand for vintage instruments is in Japan and that's where they're going. As guitar becomes more popular with the younger kids, it seems that some of the demand is dropping for vintage because the guitar heroes today play new guitars. That's not all bad. It has caused Fender and particularly Gibson to start turning out some decent products. It also gives us a good 'window of opportunity' with Hamer."

*   *   *

Ron Lira, Guitar Builder and Restoration Specialist, Honest Ron's Guitars, Oklahoma.

(1) "I am still collecting, although I'm having a harder time finding anything!! My interests include: Gibson Les Pauls, Gibson ES-335, 345, 355, Gibson mandolins, Fender Strats, Teles, Basses, Gibson Lap Steels, Fender Tweed, blond and brown amps. Martin D acoustics are also of interest to me."

(2) "The vintage market has gotten crazier! There seems no end to the amount of money people will pay for an original excellent condition instrument! I think you will see a continued rise in prices with the 'spikes' we see when a certain instrument suddenly gets popular. Guitar collecting is getting more expensive and great pieces are getting harder to find."

*   *   *

Tim Matyas, Musician, Guitar/Amplifier Repairman, Guitar Gallery, Pennsylvania.

(1) "Well, here it is 1990 and I'm still collecting! By now I thought I'd be out of it, sell all the guitars, and be rolling in dough! I'm still looking for that certain piece that I don't have, and to make matters worse, I'm getting more into collecting amps too! A big change for me personally is that I'm not that 'crazy' to buy a piece from a dealers list because these things are so expensive anymore. It used to be I'd see a guitar I wanted on a list and go crazy for it. Now I'm willing to wait to find one locally at just the 'right' deal. The vintage guitars are still out there. Most of my guitars I bought locally, finding them myself at good prices. Some I bought so long ago that they would be dirt cheap by today's standards. A lot of my friends say, 'Why don't you sell that piece, you have next to nothing into it, and make a big profit.' But that's not the way I feel about it. Almost all of my guitars I'd never be able to replace at today's costs compared to what I have into them, so why not keep them, and enjoy a great vintage guitar at a ridiculously low price? I guess I enjoy the guitars more than I would making the profits."

(2) "I always thought the market would die down since so many younger players aren't into vintage guitars, but it seems healthier and stronger than ever. Shows are springing up everywhere with fantastic turn-outs."

*   *   *

Steve Melkisethian, Angela Instruments, Maryland.

(1) "Still doing it. Moved our shop to a nice new location this year. Also dealing in vintage Hi-Fi tube gear ('50's-'60's), plastic radios, vintage TV's. Also collect vintage pens, watches, 50's furniture and plastic. Vintage Hi-Fi thing is like the guitar market was 20 years ago; I'm buying from geezers who just want to get rid of their old 'junk!' Lots of FUN!"

(2) "Prices have gone too high on many items for people with average incomes to be able to enjoy owning them. Too risky to gig with, most of 'em seem to stay in the case! Used to be a real cool diverse bunch collecting actively. Now it seems to be Japanese 'investors,' drug bums, trust fund babies, etc. Through the years I've tried to never forget the ROOT CONNECTION this vintage guitar thing has to <u>MUSIC</u>. My job as a dealer is to make as much on my stuff as I can, but I still sell stuff real cheap to young bands, try to teach them how to fix up their stuff, and anything else that helps out. I'm just as happy selling decent, cheap used utility guitars to working bands, struggling artists as I am dealing with collectors items."

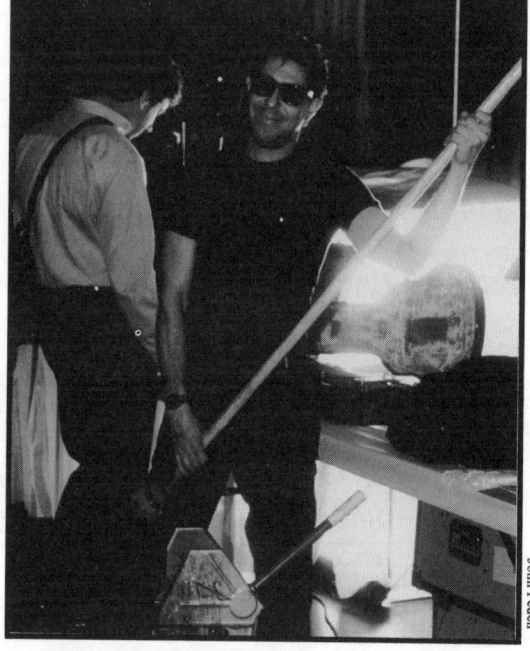

1986 was the year that Steve Melkisethian literally cleaned up at the Dallas Show.

"My favorite collectors are the guys who have something to SHARE: information about the stuff they collect, books, records, serial numbers, restoration tips, parts supplies, etc. You can tell when someone's interested in something besides money when they help you find stuff you've been looking for (in all my years in this biz, with the thousands of people I talk to, only a few have ever tried to help me find instruments, amps, parts, etc. I've been seeking for my personal use...). So tell 'em man, <u>BRING SOMETHING TO THE PARTY</u> (besides $$$), or get the___out!"

*   *   *

Marc Newman, Private Collector, Co-publisher of <u>Guitar Digest</u> Ohio.

(1) "My collecting has always been based largely on whim (my goal is to have one of every brand, at least), with that in mind, I don't think my collecting has really changed at all — I just love this stuff!"

(2) "Prices seem to be getting awfully high on things that I am not sure are really all that good. I would like to think that this trend will stop but unfortunately I don't think it will. I see nothing but growth for the vintage market — especially with the surge in foreign collecting."

* * *

Allan Potter (Montana Al), Private Collector, Montana.

(1) "No change, still searching papers and shops. Moved back to Montana and bought a bar in hopes of displaying my Instruments: current number [owned is] 225 Fender and 175 other vintage instruments including banjos, ukes, auto harps, zithers, mandolin, dobros, Nationals, old lap steels, Ricks, fiddles, etc."

(2) "I think it will keep moving up and with other newer instruments replacing the old as the old becomes out of reach price wise or availability."

* * *

Bob Reed, Private Collector, Barnet, Herts, England.

(1) At the time of completing the 1986 Questionnaire I had just moved to a new house and more or less ceased collecting from that point due to the financial drain incurred. Although it is true to say that I did buy a couple of pieces, that I just couldn't resist, over the next two years. Unfortunately, at the end of 1988, my business life took a dive, a major source of work that I had relied on for 14 years folded up, plunging me further into 'Guitar Collecting Hibernation!' The purpose of my collection changed from being an escape from the pressures of my busy working life, to being a safety valve to stop me worrying so much about when and where I would get my next job from."

"During this time, I felt something like an alcoholic who was in the process of quitting the bottle. I would avoid guitar shops, places where guitars were advertised, even avoid contact with guitar collecting friends for fear of being tempted by the thought of...'just one more guitar won't hurt!'"

"After 18 months since the partial collapse of my business, things looked pretty stable again. So recently I emerged from my 'guitar collecting hibernation' to be stunned by a scene of third rate vintage guitars with astronomical price tags!"

"I desperately searched for a collecting interest, but even old unplayable vintage junk beginners guitars had reached prices far in excess of their quality or true value."

(2) "I speak obviously from British Collector's point of view, but do get American stock lists occasionally and by comparison I can see little future for vintage guitars in the U.K. Shops regularly buy stock from the U.S.A. and mark it up at exhorbitant prices even considering import duty and tax. Commission on sale selling is common practice. Whereby a seller will state how much <u>he</u> wants for a guitar usually already unrealistic, the shop dealer will then add on 25 per cent commission and then decorate the walls of his shop with instruments that he knows full well he is not likely to sell at such prices. It costs him nothing to do this and as one dealer admitted to me 'we just like having them on the wall, punters come in to look at them and we then sell them something cheaper.'"

"Unfortunately, this affects the private sellers market....Joe Strummer sees that 'Kerrang Twang guitars' have a resprayed beaten up 62 Strat for $3500 so I'll sell mine for that....he thinks!"

"Eventually, the market has to stagnate as prices escalate to insane levels beyond the reach of normal collectors."

"The price I paid at the end of 1985 for a pristine '54 Strat from a dealer wouldn't even buy me a really beaten up pre-CBS sunburst Strat from the same dealer now. So perhaps I should be grateful and feel fortunate that I bought when I did, but I feel somewhat sad that my buying days are now over and that new collectors may not be created."

* * *

Jeff Ridolfi, Private Collector, California.

(1) and (2) "Who the Hell is Pompolini?"

Jeff Ridolfi

"While continuing to maintain an interest in vintage guitars and collecting, I find that the time and funds which I could once comfortably devote to these pursuits are no longer as available as I would like. A new job, a growing child, and some changing priorities have relegated me more toward the role of an onlooker, as opposed to a participant, in the current vintage guitar scene. I would admit that the transition has not been an easy or pleasant experience. I have also observed that I have not made the transition alone."

"My interest in vintage guitars began about 20 years ago and was not spurred by the rarity of the guitars themselves, the materials and workmanship of which they are composed, or their aesthetic qualities. Nor did I ever place a high priority on the quality of a particular guitar as an investment. Certainly, each of these things is a legitimate reason to collect. My focus, however, was primarily on the music which had and which could emanate from them. No doubt, there's a bit of nostalgia that enters the mix at this point as well. But alas, I know that one of Jimi's Strats in my hands is really nothing more than an old guitar, and it really doesn't matter how many of them I own or how much money I paid to acquire them. Some things just can't be bought."

"Nowadays, however, I really don't care to buy much of anything, and it seems difficult to predict when or if I will again become a participant in the vintage guitar market. Today, stock lists from vintage guitar dealers impart more "sticker shock" to me than information on availability, and with the rapidly rising or already high prices in evidence, guitar collecting for many has become more of a selection process than a collection process. That is, the escalation in vintage guitar prices in recent years has far outpaced the increase in disposable income of most potential buyers during the same period. As a result, more collectors are 'trading up' and shifting equities within existing collections to other guitars they now find desirable. Unfortunately, collections are not built in this fashion, only maintained, and sometimes diminished."

"However, for those who are not burdened with the problem of limited disposable income, the future of the vintage guitar market appears to be bright. Examples abound, at guitar shows, and elsewhere in the world of fine collectibles. For example, record prices have recently been paid for paintings by Van Gogh and Renoir...and Pompolini, which brings me to the title of this essay and my prediction as to the future of the vintage guitar market and the activity of guitar collecting."

"The art world has recently witnessed prices in the $70 to $80 million range for several of the works of the old masters. At least one of the major auctioneers is predicting such prices will reach and exceed $100 million in the near future as similar works of art find their way to the auction block. On the auction floor, activity is subdued but cutthroat, with many unhappy potential buyers dropping out of the bidding as prices reach previously unimagined levels."

"What's an art lover or buyer without a lot of resources going to do in a world where it takes $100 million or more just to sit in and cut the cards? Well, thank goodness for Pompolini. You see, very few connoisseurs of art even know who Pompolini is. Even worse, very few art auctioneers know who Pompolini is, and, until recently, they didn't care either. But, in the superheated market of fine art, you've just got to have vision. Let the buying frenzy begin!"

"I can't claim the title of this essay as my own. It is actually a quote from an employee of a major auction house. It seems the crowd was still catching its breath over the record price which had just been paid for a fine old painting. Later in the festivities, a Pompolini original was offered for sale to the feverish mob with an accompanying minimum bid of $10,000. A silence fell over the crowd. Then suddenly, as if from nowhere, a bidder in the crowd sounded '$70,000.' With a stark note of disbelief in his voice, the auctioneer cried 'WHAT!?' in response to the bid, seeming to question the legitimacy of the offer (and offeree), but immediately slammed the gavel to the podium, closing the bidding before things got out of hand (and the bidder changed his mind)."

"This sort of attitude toward public service by the auctioneer is to be commended. At least, there is still a glimmer of hope remaining for those who have yet to acquire an original Pompolini for their own and who are further strapped with limited funds. Isn't the art world great!?"

"To make light of such a situation is to mock it. And, it is also very easy for me to do since I am not in the market for fine art. However, the similarity between the current state of the market for fine art and vintage guitars does cause me some consternation since vintage guitars (and things related) is my hobby, my only hobby. As such, vintage guitaring has provided me with an enjoyable diversion from my normal activities and a lot of good times over the years."

"I refuse to accept the notion of some that it is 'the customer' or 'the collector' who is responsible for the current state of the vintage guitar market. Such generic descriptions of a small market segment are a disservice to and a misrepresentation of the majority who have spent recent years on the sidelines of the vintage guitar market. For us, even those 'Pompolinis' out there are fast becoming, if not already, instruments out of reach. Like the auctioneer, I find myself wondering why."

"The fact remains that the current vintage market is made or broken by the current market participants. The credit or disdain for this basic truth should properly be doled out to those to whom it is due, if indeed that is one's mission."

"In all likelihood, effective market demand for true vintage guitars will continue to decline as fewer market participants can make the cut financially. From my limited point of view, this is an unfortunate circumstance because the interaction with others having similar interests and the 'thrill of the hunt' are some of the things I enjoy most about vintage guitaring... these things, and the music. Guitars are not paintings. Some things just can't be bought... or sold."

*   *   *

Jay Scott, Author, Guitar Historian, Nutty Jazz Guitars, New York.

(1)"I didn't participate in the first survey. I genuinely feel that collecting/buying/owning/playing (vintage) guitars is a phenomenon of a confluence of discreet factors, <u>viz</u> the mercantile, an aesthetic component, an inherent musical direction, some sort of psychological aggrandizement, a dexterity-manual aspect (so many players refer to holding the instrument in their hands as emotionally satisfying), the need to hoard, and some kind of eccentric-pariah-like portion. For instance, my father was a drummer and although my contact with him was marginal, the transference must have been very strong (maybe stronger!). I seem to demonstrate an early artistic penchant, holding things in my hands was very satisfying. I can remember falling asleep so often holding a guitar. When I grew up I needed to make a living (marginal), I was never a joiner, maybe all this predisposes to... a life with the vintage American guitar."

(2)"The vintage guitar market has established itself as an international market dealing in Americana, as valid and solid as the antiques or any of the other commodities market. 'Strong' doesn't define this market; it's an international futures and commodities exchange."

*   *   *

Richard Smith, Musician, Author, Vintage Guitar Historian/Authority, California.

(1)"I still have a nice collection of pre-CBS Fenders and Rickenbacker twelve-strings. Aside from the twelve-strings, which I acquired a taste for, I like the same guitars I liked in the early 1970's. My new interests include guitar catalogs and original rayon Hawaiian shirts! Aloha!"

(2)"Guitar collecting will continue. The vintage market will continue as well. Moreover, the guitars that thirty and forty year olds collect now will still set the standards for most collectors. However, a new generation of collectors is emerging, too. Instruments the older collectors ignored in the 1970's, like B.C. Riches and Dean guitars, will probably have their day. Who knows what else? I remember seeing Charvel Van Halen guitars at a late 1970's NAMM show. Where are they now? Some kid in Iowa probably has six of them under his bed next to his stash of Playboys."

*   *   *

Gilbert Southworth, Southworth Guitars, Washington, D.C.

(1) Q. How have your collecting activities changed since your participation in the survey? A. "I have more guitars." Q. Where are you now? A. "Earth." Q. Still collecting? A. "Like crazy." Q. Current interests, etc? A. "Bicycling, golf."

(2) Q. What are your thoughts or predictions as to the future of the vintage guitar market and the activity of guitar collecting? A. "It's all happ'nin.'"

* * *

Thomas A. Van Hoose, Private Collector, Author, Guitar Historian, Texas.

(1) "Since my last participation in your survey, things continue to change and evolve for me and my collecting activities. First, my guitar collection of Super 400 appears to be complete at the present time. Second, my forthcoming book, The Gibson Super 400 - Art of the Fine Guitar (San Francisco, Miller-Freeman, 1991 in press) will be published in the summer of 1991. Much of my activity regarding vintage instrument collecting is focused on the completion of this book and its publication. Third, I have started a small 'second collection' of carved-top instruments that represent the peak of vintage instrument quality across different brands of instruments. That is, I have compiled a very focused small collection of natural finish, noncutaway carved-top guitars consisting of a D'Angelico New Yorker, a Gibson Super 400, an Epiphone Emperor, and a Stromberg Master 400. In addition, I am slowly compiling a 'counterpoint' to these instruments, as made by current luthiers and manufacturers. This part of the 'second collection' currently consists of a D'Aquisto Excel, a Benedetto Fratello and a Heritage Super Eagle (all natural finish, cutaway, and made for me), and a 1969 L5C that belonged to my guitar teacher. My current interests include finishing my book on the Super 400, refining and upgrading my Super 400 collection and keeping the collection in a good state of repair and playability, and refining this 'second collection,' and playing music again in a variety of contexts."

(2) "The future of the vintage guitar market appears very bright to me. There will be a plethora of books emerging within the next year on various aspects of guitar collecting, which will serve to inform the public and certainly create additional interest in the vintage guitar market. Such publications usually tend to push the prices of vintage guitars in an upward direction. I also predict that the activity of guitar collecting will continue to evolve, both in terms of the number of collectors and their increasing sophistication. It appears to me that the guitar, both vintage and new, is entering a new 'boom' phase in which interest in these vintage instruments will be increasingly widespread."

* * *

James Werner, Fender Collector, Iowa.

(1) "I've been buying a lot less and gathering more factual information about what I have. I don't have much 'sense' and even fewer 'dollars' and simply won't pay collector prices — even though I'm a collector. I haven't been able to afford guitars and amps for several years. I get good reports from all over about nice items for realistic prices, but once they hit mainstream collecting — they become rather inaccessible for me. It's supply + demand = price."

"I work a lot on the Fender instrument serial number list and can obtain pictures and information on pieces that I'll never own — that's very satisfying in itself. I also give out information and put people together for their want/for sale requirements — that's important also — everyone gains. My currents interests include reading, music, movies."

(2) "The market will continue to climb — the 'soft spots' (lower priced) will rise. I don't see anything going crazy upward — just steady upward trend in everything from paper goods to parts to complete instruments and amps. Originality and condition determine money value. Vintage instrument collecting is becoming a wealthy only pastime. It is nice seeing more publications and information being published so you can find out about what you can't afford."

* * *

Bart Wittrock, Rockin' Robin Guitars, Texas.

(1) "I play custom built Robin guitars with vintage features because I don't want equity in my 'playing' guitars — vintage guitars are whores — only $$$! Since there really is no 'right' reason to collect, there are some real surprises as to what people want and what they will pay for what they want! What seems crazy to one person may be a steal to another — unlike coins! — values are very established for anyone who can read. Guitars and related instruments vary dramatically."

"I'm free! I found out that once you mature as a player and you have a guitar with proper (for you) neck, pickups and color (i.e. your attitude is right) you can kick ass on a '59 or '89 guitar! P.S. Send old 'KOA' wood ukeleles. I collect for FUN!

(2) "Gibsons will appreciate like a comet.
    Fenders — up but stable.
        Market in general —healthy increase!"

* * *

Tom Wittrock, Third Eye Music, Missouri.

(1) "My collecting of '58-'60 Sunburst Les Pauls has increased and my collection has improved dramatically, It is probably the finest in the world."

(2) "The future of the vintage market and guitar collecting is very complicated. Foreign interest in the last 10 years has dramatically boosted the market. Americans are often outbid on fine collectors pieces. Currently the foreign market wants supreme collectible pieces of the highest caliber and lots of low end marginally collectible guitars. Despite all the bitching and moaning in the guitar press about prices and foreigners, there are plenty of good guitars to be had. But the finest (most collectible of all) guitars are definitely dwindling in number."

"I find the average collector that I come in contact with is much different than ten years ago. Despite the fact that there is more information available (and more accurate) they are generally less educated about old guitars and they don't seem to want to learn. In my own specialty ('58-'60 Sunburst Les Pauls) I deal with some of the most expensive guitars in the vintage market place. I am constantly confronted by potential buyers (of $20,000. guitars) who have very little understanding or appreciation of what they are buying. They have to rely heavily on the opinions of others. They are overly concerned about whether they can resell the guitar in the future, but can't make that determination for themselves. I find this [to be] true with most high priced guitars, and to a lesser extent [with] almost all used guitar purchases. I feel if the average collector were to show enough interest to learn the fine points of collectible guitars, variations of models they seek, and study the market, they will be better equipped to make their own decisions and the market will improve dramatically."

"In recent years I have read a lot of negative press about guitar dealers. They are depicted as people only concerned with making huge profits and to hell with the consumer. Most vintage dealers are also players and collectors. Some of them (like myself) are among the most avid collectors in the world. Vintage guitar prices are not controlled in any way by a group of people. They are controlled by the same basic market factors that control almost all commodities — supply and demand. People will not pay more than they are willing to pay for any non-necessity, and it's crazy to expect someone to sell an item for less than they know they can get for it. "Dave and Mike are walking along when Dave finds a twenty dollar bill. Mike says, 'You've got nothing in it, sell it to me for ten dollars!'" Is Dave crazy for holding out for more when he knows he can get it? It makes no difference what he paid for it. Guitars are worth what someone will give — no more, no less! Most dealers enhance the market — there wouldn't be a market at all without dealers. Most are unbelievably honest and trustworthy. The history of the giant Texas guitar shows (Spring and Fall) bear this out.

"The vintage guitar market will continue as long as guitars are popular, but it will take some effort for it to improve. Education about vintage guitars is essential and the best learning place by far is guitar shows. Even if one is not buying or selling, the educational value (and fun) of vintage shows are invaluable. I still have some optimism for the 1990's and the 21st century."

*   *   *

The collectors' responses provide fascinating reading for the vintage guitar enthusiast. Despite an earlier promise not to "categorize or analyze," a few impressions are impossible to disregard. More than one individual that had grown weary of collecting and dropped out found a renewed interest in time. It appears that the "mania" may diminish, but the intrigue sustains. The whole constellation of factors that account for a person's initial entry into the field are so deeply rooted to the individual's existence and identity that a total rejection of all collecting interests seems to be a very unlikely occurrence. This is fortunate for those of us who will benefit from the additional publications generated as a result of the continued efforts of the enthusiast writers. Virtually all of the survey participants/authors have new titles in process. The balance of individuals that remain "hooked" on collecting may take into consideration the old adage on accomplishing long life: develop a chronic disorder, and learn how to take care of it.

The collectors have expressed differing opinions as to the future of the vintage guitar market, but the general perception of a vital field is evidenced. The dramatic changes that have occurred in just the last five years or so are nicely illustrated by the collectors, and document the fact of a maturing and developing guitar collecting enterprise.

The Guitar Collector Survey has explored the psychology of guitar collecting by an investigation of the collectors' comments. The venture has been enjoyable and meaningful to the author, but has it produced unique and original findings? Probably not. Several years after the initial investigation was completed the **clever** guys at Guitar Digest unearthed some eloquent comments on collecting which predated the primary insights derived from the survey by over 60 years! Somewhat consoling was the fact that the individual was also a psychologist. Actually Joseph Jastrow was an important figure and happened to be the first candidate to graduate from a Ph.D. program in psychology in the United States. Dr. Jastrow completed his degree at Johns Hopkins in the late 1800's, and in Keeping Mentally Fit (1928) he commented on "the mania for collecting":

"Collecting, like most hobbies, serves an admirable purpose. It is an offset to business, and even when it comes to be a business, it retains the sentiment of attachment. The objects collected have a value beyond their intrinsic worth; the collector gets a thrill, first in finding the rare and unusual, next in the joy of possession, also in outdoing his rival and in shrewd bargaining."

"No one is in business for his health, but he is in collecting for his health, his mental health and the satisfaction he gets out of his own growth in the art of collecting."

"Collecting is also educational. Many a boy learns as much geography from his stamp collection as from the textbook. Museums form an important aid to education. Collections of art and human industry keep us in touch with our past; collections of science unroll the great panorama of nature. Both enlarge interest, develop appreciation."

"But, seeing a collection and owning one are different experiences, like listening to music and playing an instrument. Music is kept alive by amateur performers. 'Amateur' is a French way of saying 'lover'; collecting is something you do for the love of it, through the joy of possession and the sense of being richer — more in knowledge than in goods — enter into it."

"Collectors as a class form a gentle and agreeable variety of human beings, departing amicably, if at all, from sanity. It is only occasionally that collecting amounts to a mania that somewhat disturbs the rule of good sense — which is the standard test of mental fitness — or shades over into a costly pastime."

Guitar collecting can be a "costly pastime," and the proof of whether the collectors always abide by the "rule of good sense" is somewhat lacking. But, despite its imperfections and side effects (such as Old Guitar Mania), guitar collecting is truly a noble venture and worthy of the considerable personal commitment that these individuals have made to the preservation and appreciation of vintage guitars.

Gibson ES350. 1951. Perfect Condition. Note Curley maple, P. 90's.

'62 Vintage Stratocaster

Amp: Vox A.C. 30 top boost with blue speakers, circa 1963

Front Row: Guitars L to R -November '59 Strat serial #47331 blonde re-finish/ July '62 Strat, serial #87555 original Fiesta Red/ September '64 Burns Marvin serial # 6937 one of only 300 Burns Marvins made original white-tortoiseshell./December '54 Strat serial #6800 original amber sunburst one piece figured ash body./February '63 Jaguar serial #99203 original Sonic Blue

Back row: Guitars L to R - '63 Burns Sonic Cherry Red/ '64 Burns Shortscale - serial #3747 Jazz black-redsunburst/ June '82 U.S.A. vintage re-issue Fiesta Red early batch - mint unplayed serial # V000900, one of the first three samples shipped to U.K. original sales receipt dated November 19, 1982. / Cherry Red '60 Burns Artist Bass/ February '62 Fender Duo-Sonic serial #87360 original maroon, red, yellow sunburst.

Front: Circa 1963 Vox Echo Unit shadows model tape and valve-6 playback heads.

The first acoustic Fender, was presented to J. Fred McCord by Leo Fender in the early 1960's. This information is contained inside the sound hole and was signed by Leo Fender.

Bill Carson, July 7-90.
Holding a 35th Anniversary Strat, Serial #100

-Appendix A-

Bill Blackburn, Ph.D.
Psychologist

<u>GUITAR COLLECTOR QUESTIONNAIRE</u>

Name_____ Copyright © 1984 by Bill Blackburn

Occupation and brief biographical sketch_____
_____
_____
_____
_____
_____

Age_____   Sex   M   F

How many years have you collected guitars?_____

How many guitars are in your personal collection?_____

What kind of guitars do you collect?_____
_____

Do you have a favorite vintage or non-vintage guitar that you are especially attached to?_____ If so: make_____ model_____, year_____and why this guitar is so special to you_____
_____

Listed below are various important elements of vintage guitars. Please rate them in terms of significance for <u>yourself</u>. Place a <u>1</u> on the line beside the most important element, a <u>2</u> beside the next most important, etc.

_____ appearance   _____ historical significance

_____ "feel"   _____ association with a famous player

_____ sound   _____ exclusivity, status appeal

_____ craftmanship   _____ investment potential

Others? List and rate _____

_____

_____

Do you play guitar? _____ If so, please rate your ability on the following scale (circle the appropriate number)

        Poor 1 2 3 4 5 6 7 Excellent

What style(s) of music do you play? _____

How many hours per week would you say you spend in activities (reading, phone calls, visiting music shops or private owners, etc.) related to your personal guitar collection? _____

Circle the answers that most accurately reflect how important guitar collecting is to you:

1) How "into" guitar collecting would you say you are?

    Not much at all   a little   a lot   very "into" it

2) How important to you is being involved in some collecting activity every day?

    not important at all   not very important   Important   very important

3) How important to your life in general (well-being, mood, relaxation, self-satisfaction, etc.) is you personal interest in guitar collecting?

    not important at all   not very important   Important   very important

Please answer the following questions on a separate sheet of paper.

1) What is your personal definition of a guitar collector?

2) How did you initially become interested in collecting guitars?

3) Why is or is not guitar collecting an important part of your life?

4) What does guitar collecting do for you? (Describe psychological, emotional, financial, social factors, etc.)

5) Where is your collection going? (What are you looking for? What is your ultimate goal, etc)

6) What is your preferred method of locating old guitars for sale?

7) What do you find to be the most enjoyable aspect of collecting?

8) What do you find to be the most annoying aspect of collecting and the vintage guitar field in general?

9) Describe the reasons behind your preference for vintage guitars.

10) What do you think this "old guitar mania" is all about? (What causes it, where did it come from, specific "symptoms" you have observed, your evaluation of it, etc.).

11) Where is the vintage guitar market headed?

12) Any other comments you would like to make regarding guitar collecting or old guitar ownership?

Consent and Release Agreement

I hereby consent to and authorize the use of my name and responses given on the Guitar Collector Questionnaire to Bill Blackburn to be used in a future publication on guitar collectors. I volunteer this information without financial compensation for the stated purpose.

I am over 21 years of age. _____ Yes or No

_____   _____
        Signature   Date

Witnessed by:_____
                Signature of Witness

APPENDIX B

BE-BOP-A-BLACK STRAT

A guitar can conceivably earn historic significance in at least two basic ways: what it is, or who played it. This story of one of the first custom-color Strats is an example of a "crossover" guitar which qualifies as both a vintage guitar and an item of rock 'n roll memorabilia. This particular guitar played a simultaneous role in guitar and music history.

Those two threads of history converged naturally, as the development of rock 'n roll music occurred at roughly the same time as the emergence of the Fender Stratocaster guitar. Who could have predicted in 1955, when this black Stratocaster was purchased, that rock music as well as the Fender Strat would both achieve such enormous, lasting popularity? Perhaps Howard Reed, Jr.

The late Howard Allen Reed, Jr. (1937-1981) ordered this guitar through J. Fred McCord of McCord Music Company in Dallas, Texas. McCord was Howard's guitar teacher in the late forties and owned one of the largest Fender dealerships in the fifties. Howard requested a special-order "custom color" black Stratocaster before such finishes were first offered in the 1956 Fender catalog. The standard finish for the Stratocaster at that time was, of course, the two-color sunburst. In 1954 and 1955, a few solid-color production Stratocasters were released for promotional purposes in connection with the requests of established artists. The most-oft-cited example from the year of the Strat's introduction (1954) is a metallic gold guitar owned by Eldon Shamblin who played with Bob Wills and his Texas Playboys. At least two other red examples existed and were the personal instruments of Bill Carson and Pee Wee Crayton, as documented by Fender historian Richard R. Smith. Thus, Howard's black guitar was not the first custom color Strat, but it was perhaps one of the earliest ordered from outside the factory, and certainly one of the few in existence with clear documentation of authenticity. The special request for a black Stratocaster was no doubt facilitated by J. Fred McCord's standing as a Fender dealer and his personal relationships with Fender officials.

A few years after Howard bought the black Strat, he was playing it on **The Big D** Jamboree radio music program, a show which first aired in the early forties, similar in concept to the Grand Ole Opry. The program was broadcast live and nationwide via CBS radio from the Sportatorium in Dallas, Texas. Naomi, Howard's mother, continues the story: "Howard was playing for different singers at the Sportatorium in Dallas — a country show each night. Gene Vincent's manager approached Howard to be lead guitarist for Gene's band. Howard wasn't sure he wanted to travel, so he played with Gene's band on some shows he had booked around Dallas." According to Howard's mother, Gene Vincent called Howard after he and the Blue Caps left Dallas for the next show in Canada and convinced him to become a permanent member of the group. James Werner, the seldom-seen but often-referred-to Fender collector, confirms this story in a circa-1980 phone conversation he had with Howard, "If I remember correctly," Jim states, "Howard joined Vincent in the spring of 1958. Vincent's first guitarist was Cliff Gallup, but it was Johnny Meeks that Howard replaced for a period of time. (Howard said Meeks 'defined' the Vincent sound)."

"After Howard was contacted, he went from Dallas to Winnipeg, Canada, rehearsed five to six hours and did his first professional show that night. Howard used the black Strat on stage and in the studio — he was getting up a list of what he played on for me, but he list was never completed due to his untimely and tragic death. After Vincent, Howard was with Buddy Knox, Jimmy Bowen and a host of others. He said he was also a session guitarist at Motown for a period."

The guitar was played by Howard in 48 states and Canada during the late fifties. Howard wrote, "For all its scars and scratches, it **is** a working man's guitar and it **has** been all over hell and back."

Howard Reed, Jr. died of a stroke in 1981 at the age of 43. In late 1979 he had obtained written documentation on his guitar from J. Fred McCord, which included a copy of the original ledger sheet from

B Blackburn

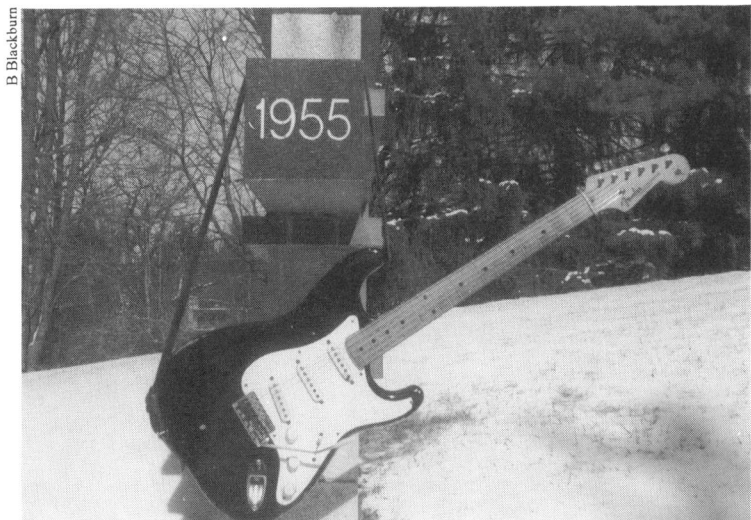

The Howard Reed Strat - No question about the year or color

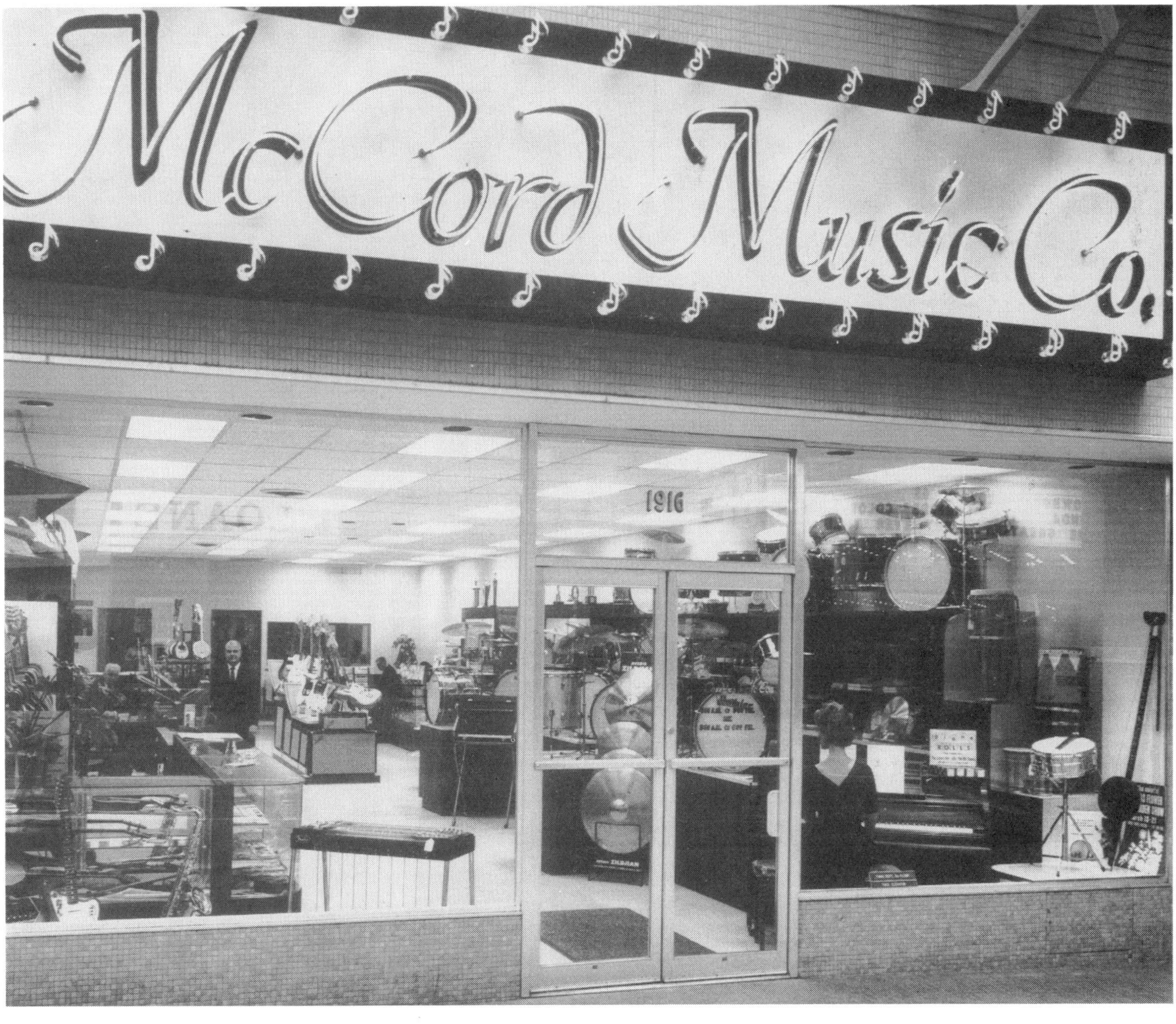

Courtesy of J. Fred McCord

McCord Music Co. where Howard Reed took guitar lessons and had his teacher and store owner, J. Fred McCord, order the custom color black Strat. McCord opened the downtown location in 1945, and Howard's guitar arrived at this three story building in the heart of Dallas just in time for Christmas, 1955.

Leo Fender and J. Fred McCord in Leo's workshop (Circa1973-4). McCord sold Fender's products from the first Broadcasters to the later G & L's. Fender and McCord were contemporaries and both pioneers in the guitar business serving the complimentary roles of the creative/manufacturing and the musical/merchandising respectively.

J. Fred McCord standing in the center of his store in 1965 with some of his staff. McCord, being one of the first and largest Fender dealers, sold many professionals their instruments. Trini Lopez and Ray Price bought their first guitars there. Buddy Holly, Chuck Berry, Carl Perkins, Ike and Tina Turner, Chet Atkins, Freddie King and countless others were customers.

McCord Music Company

1916 ELM STREET, DALLAS, TEXAS 75201 • 741-3483

November 28, 1979

Mr. Howard Reed
902 McDonald Dr.
Garland, Texas 75041

Dear Howard:

I am enclosing a copy of our ledger sheet which shows that you purchased a Fender Black Stratocaster Serial No. 10041 and case from this company on Dec. 17, 1955.

This letter should serve for anyone who may be interested.

Sincerely,

McCORD MUSIC COMPANY

J. Fred McCord
President

JFM:yz

encl.

-Appendix C-

Bill Blackburn, Ph.D.
Psychologist

Guitar Collector Questionaire
(Update)
Copyright © 1990 by Bill Blackburn

1. How have your collecting activities changed since your participation in the survey? Where are you now?, Still collecting?, Current Interests, etc?

   _____

   _____

   _____

2. What are your thoughts or predictions as to the future of the vintage guitar market and the activity of guitar collecting?

   _____

   _____

   _____

Please use the back of this as needed, or attach additional sheet.

Consent and Release Agreement

I hereby consent to and authorize the use of my name, photographs submitted, and responses given on the Guitar Collector Questionaire to Bill Blackburn to be used in a future publication on guitar collecting. I volunteer this information without financial compensation for the stated purpose and realize that materials submitted can not be returned.

I am over 21 years of age _____ Yes or No.

_____   _____
          Signature   Date

Witnessed by: _____
              Signature of Witness

Bill Blackburn, Ph.D.
Psychologist

GUITAR WIDOWS SAY...   **"OLD GUITARS SMELL!"**

Is a Bronco a collector's guitar?

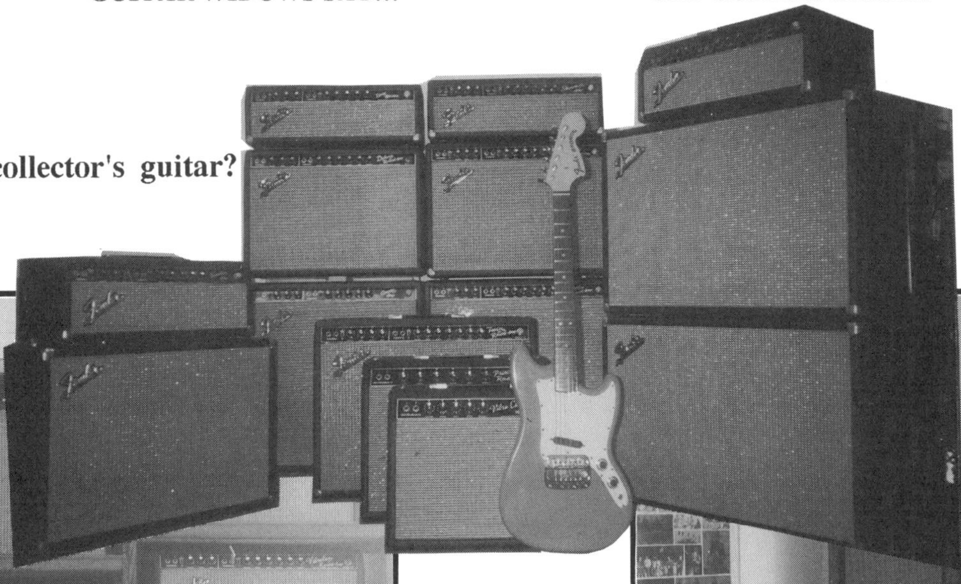

"Black face" Fender Reverb Amps.    **Fender "black face" amps and Precision bass**

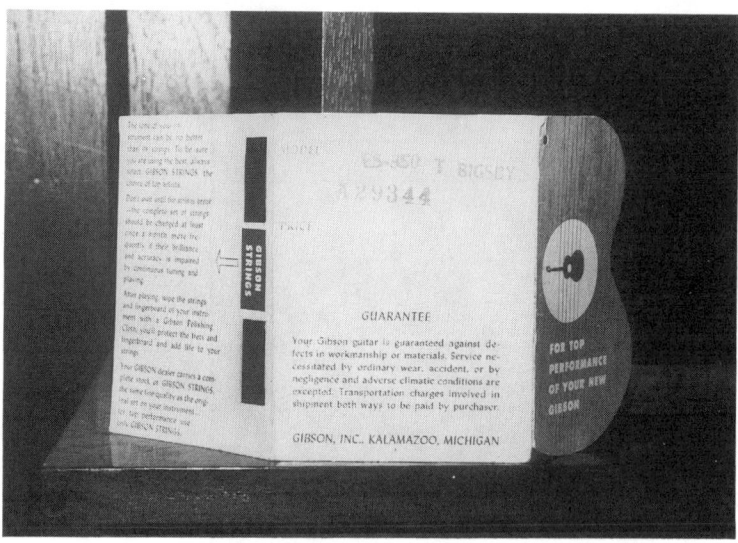

Gibson, 1959. ES-350T and original tag with Specified Bigsby.

Gretsch 6120 Nashville

Teles and Tweed

BIBLIOGRAPHY

Bacon, Tony and Paul Day. The Guru's Guitar Guide. Track Record Publishing.

Bellson, Julius. The Gibson Story.

Blasquiz, Klaus. The Fender Bass Book. Hal Leonard. (In Press)

Brozman, Bob. The History of National Guitars. Centerstream.

Bulli, John. Guitar History: Volume 2. Gibson S.G. The Bold Strummer Ltd.

Crocker, Dave, John Brinkman and Larry Briggs. Guitars, Guitars, Guitars. All American Music Publishers.

Day, Paul. The Burns Book. P. D. Publishing

Duchossoir, A.R. The Fender Stratocaster. Mediapresse/Hal Leonard.

Duchossoir, A.R. The Fender Telecaster. Hal Leonard. (In Press)

Duchossoir, A.R. Gibson Electrics Vol. 1. Mediapresse/Hal Leonard.

Duchossoir, A.R. Guitar Identification. Mediapresse/Hal Leonard.

Evans, Tom and Mary Ann. Guitars from the Renaissance to Rock. Paddinton Press Ltd.

Gruhn, George and Walter Carter. Gruhn's Guide to Vintage Guitars. GPI Books, Miller Freeman Publications.

Gruhn, George and Douglas B. Green. Ray Accuff's Musical Collection. WSM, Inc.

Hartman, Robert. Guitars and Mandolins in America, Featuring the Larson's Creations. Maurer and Co.

Iwanade, Yasuhiko with Strat story by Richard Smith. Stratocaster. Centerstream.

Korinn, Allan; Welding, Pete; Forte, Dan; Santoro, Gene. The Guitar. Quill.

Longworth, Mike. Martin Guitars: A History. Four Maples Press.

Mosely, Willie G. Classic Guitars USA: A Primer. Centerstream.

Schmidt, Paul William. Acquired of The Angler: The Lives and Times of John D'Angelico and James L. D'Acquisto. Scarecrow Press.

Schnepel, Norbert and Lemme, Helmuth. Electric Guitars Made in Germany. Musik-Verlag Schnepel-Lemme OHG.

Scott, Jay. <u>The Guitars of the Fred Gretsch Company</u>. Centerstream.

Smith, Richard R. <u>The Complete History of Rickenbacker Guitars</u> Centerstream.

Stewart, John G. and Keith Wait. <u>Marketwright Vintage Blue Book</u>. Marketwright.

Tsumura, Akira. Guitars. <u>The Tsumura Collection.</u> Kodansha International Ltd.

Van Hoose, Thomas. <u>The Gibson Super 400 Art of The Fine Guitar.</u> MillerFreeman.

Wheeler, Tom. <u>American Guitars.</u> Harper and Row.

Wheeler, Tom. <u>The Guitar Book</u>. Harper and Row.

Willcutt, J. Robert and Ball, Kenneth R. <u>The Musical Instrument Collector</u>. The Bold Strummer Ltd.

Yasuda, Mac. <u>The Vintage Guitar, Volume One</u>. Shinko Music Pub. Co., Ltd.

Yasuda, Mac. <u>The Vintage Guitar, Volume Two</u>. Shinko Music Pub. Co., Ltd.

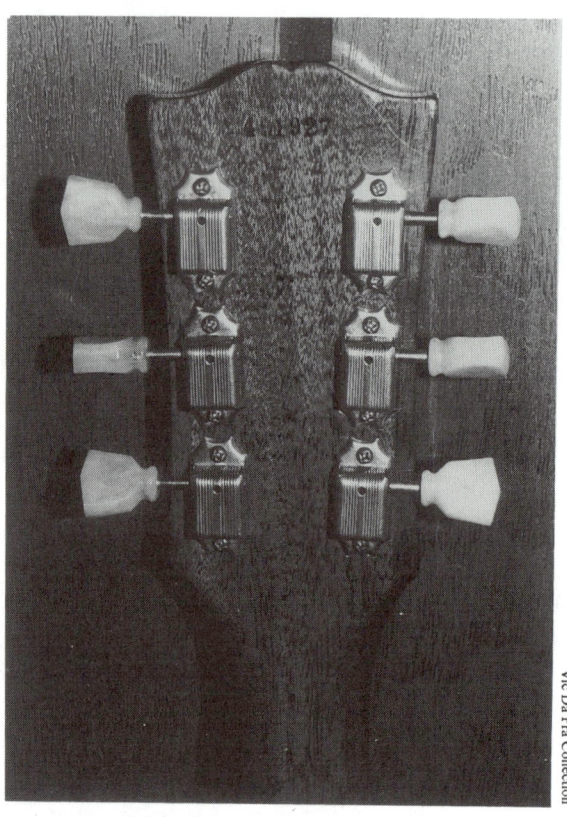

Vic Da Pra Collection

1954 Gibson Les Paul gold top; P 90's, barrel Knobs, stop tailpiece/bridge combination. Note "Inked on" serial number 4-1927 on back of headstock

Guitar Quiz!

Can you correctly identify the name and correct year of these guitars? If so, send your answers to the publisher.

Survey Participants/Guitar Dealers, listed in order of appearance in text

George Gruhn
Gruhn Guitars, Inc.
410 Broadway
Nashville, TN 37203

Steve Melkisethian
Angela Instruments
8600 Foundry St.
Box 2043
Savage, MD 20763

Vic Da Pra
Tim Matyas
Guitar Gallery
113 E. McMurray Rd.
McMurray PA 15317

Bart Wittrock
Rockin' Robin'
3619 S. Shepherd
Houston, TX 77098

Tom Van Hoose
Van Hoose Vintage Instruments, Inc.
1509 Main St.
Suite 801
Dallas, Tx 75201

Norm Harris
Norman's Rare Guitars
19300 Vanowen St.
Reseda, CA 91335

Ron Lira
Honest Ron's Guitars
1129 N. May Ave.
Oklahoma City, OK 73107

Tom Wittrock
Third Eye Music, Inc.
1904-A E. Meadowmere
Springfield, MO 65804

John Sprung
American Guitar Center
2446 Reedie Dr. Suite 9
Wheaton, MD 20902

Greg Golden
Bizarre Guitar
2677 Oddie Blvd.
Reno, NV 89512

Gil Southworth
Southworth Guitars
7845 Old Georgetown Rd.
Bethesda, MD 20814

C. William Kaman II
Kaman Music Corporation
P. O. Box 507
Bloomfield, CT 06002

Brian Fischer
Ear Craft
14 Fourth St.
Dover, NH 03820

Skip Henderson
City Lights Music
139 Easton Ave.
New Brunswick, NJ 08901

Paul Day
Sound Investments
45 Church Road
Newton Abbot
Devon T Q 12 1AL
England

Jay Scott
Nutty Jazz Guitars
Box 1122
Canal Street Station
New York, NY 10013-1122

Books for the Collector
from CENTERSTREAM Publishing
P.O. Box 5450 - Fullerton, CA 92635   Phone/fax (714) 779-9390

Gretsch – The Guitars of the Fred Gretsch Co.
by Jay Scott
Centerstream Publications
This is the comprehensive, must-own owner's or collector's manual for any Gretsch fan. It uncovers the history of the guitars through 32 pages of color photos, hundreds of black & white photos, and forewords by Fred Gretsch, George Harrison, Randy Bachman, Brian Setzer and Duane Eddy. It contains 30 chapters covering each Gretsch model in depth and a section of patent numbers and drawings for collectors. Find out what makes the essential "Rockabilly" guitar such a collector's item and such an icon of popular music history.
_____00000142 286 pages..........................$35.00

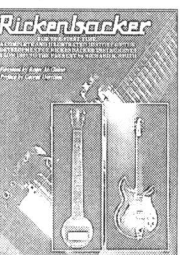

Rickenbacker
by Richard Smith
This 256-page soft-cover book gives a complete and illustrated history of the development of Rickenbacker instruments from 1931 to the present. RICKENBACKER is the only book of its kind to chronicle the history of the company who in 1931 introduced electric instruments to the world. The book provides information and full color photos of the many artists who have used and are using Rickenbacker instruments. Rickenbacker collectors will find their book invaluable as it contains recently discovered accurate facts previously unavailable to researchers.
_____00000098 256 pages..........................$29.95

The History & Artistry Of National Resonator Instruments
by Bob Brozman
Centerstream Publishing
These beautiful instruments have long been a favorite with musicians. This book is a history, source book and owner's manual for players and fans which covers the facts and figures necessary for serious collectors. In addition to many black and white historical photos, there is also a 32-page color section highlighting models. The book covers the company's full history, specific styles and models of all instruments, Hawaiian, Blues, and Jazz artists who have used Nationals, a history of their advertising, set-up and maintenance, and much more. Appendixes include serial numbers for all instruments, a company chronology and a Hawaiian Artist Discography. 296 pages.
_____00000154 Softcover $35.00

Old Guitar Mania
by Bill Blackburn
Centerstream Publications
This guide to vintage guitar collecting helps you get started, build and maintain a guitar collection with advice and personal commentary from the leading collectors and authorities in the world. Complete with lots of valuable photos, a handy guitar terminology glossary, and a bibliography for further study.
_____00000141 88 pages..........................$10.95

Guitar Legends – The Evolution of the Guitar from Fender to G&L
by George Fullerton
Centerstream Publishing
The name Fender has become synonymous with guitars. The work of Leo Fender revolutionized the instrument and has influenced nearly every modern guitarist. This book by Leo's best friend and partner in G&L examines the life of the man behind these instruments. It features photos (including 16 pages of color!) never before published. You'll see the barn where Leo was born, the first Fender plant, the earliest instruments he created, and many other rare photos.
_____00000156 112 pages..........................$24.95

STAR GUITARS – GUITARS & PLAYERS THAT HAVE HELPED SHAPE MODERN MUSIC
by Neville Marten
Centerstream Publications
Star Guitars looks at the relationships between the guitars & their players that have made music what it is today. Features 102 color pages & interesting accounts of great musicians and the guitar companies that forged the way into the future: Fender, Gibson, Gretsch, Martin, as well as international manufacturers like John Birch, Burns, Hofner, Warwick, and Zemaitis. Written by *Guitarist* magazine editor Neville Marten, with a foreword by Gary Moore.
00000168................................$24.95

Drum Collecting

Guide To Vintage Drums
by John Aldridge
Centerstream Publications
Written by John Aldridge, publisher of *Not So Modern Drummer*, this in an essential guide for collectors-to-be that want to shop around, or for current collectors to discover drums outside of their area of interest. Includes many photos and the following chapters: The Evolution Of The Drumset, The Cymbal Makers, American Drum Companies, Collectable Drums, Where To Find Vintage Drums, and Restoring without Destroying.
_____00000167 ....$24.95

History Of The Ludwig Drum Company
by Paul William Schmidt
Centerstream Publications
Discover one of America's greatest contributions to the music world – the drumset – by exploring the Ludwig Drum Company. This unique publication uses extensive interviews with the Ludwigs and photos from their personal collections to recall the origins, development and tools of the craft. You'll also discover why the best drummers – Ringo Starr, Joe Morello, Danny Gottlieb, and more – use Ludwigs. Over 150 photos and illustrations make this an invaluable reference source for all drummers.
_____00000132............................$29.95

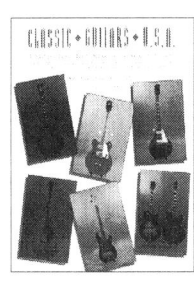

Classic Guitars U.S.A. A Primer For The Vintage Guitar Collector
Willie G. Mosely
Foreword by Stan Jay
Centerstream Publications
This is a book for anyone who loves guitars – whether you just want to learn more about them and their history, or if you are tempted to enter the world of collecting. It includes descriptions of over 125 brand names and over 540 photos, as well as sections on guitar terminology and parts information. You will also learn how to recognize counterfeits and forgeries.
$19.95 • 9x12 •   HL00000139   • 0-9317-5952-8 •

The Complete History Of The Leedy Drum Company
by Rob Cook
Centerstream Publications
This is the fascinating story of professional drummer, inventor, and industrialist Ulysses Leedy and his apartment-based drum company that became the world's largest manufacturer of percussion equipment. Features many photos documenting the company's interesting history. A must for all collectors and drum enthusiasts!
_____00000160..............................$29.95

Leedy Drum Topics
Compiled by Rob Cook
The company news magazine from 1923 to 1941, great drum history, 488 pages. $29.95

Ludwig Drum Catalog
reprint of the company's FIRST catalog of 1912. $6.50